Bride at Ten,
Mother at Fifteen

Bride at Ten, Mother at Fifteen

FORTHCOMING TITLES

Bride at Ten,
Mother at Fifteen

AUTOBIOGRAPHY OF AN UNKNOWN INDIAN WOMAN

Sethu Ramaswamy

Namita Gokhale Editions
Roli Books

This edition first published in 2003
Namita Gokhale Editions
An imprint of
Roli Books Pvt. Ltd.
M-75, G.K. II Market
New Delhi 110 048
Phones: ++91 (011) 2921 2271, 2921 2782
2921 0886; Fax: ++91 (011) 2921 7185
E-mail: roli@vsnl.com, Website: rolibooks.com

Also at
Varanasi, Agra, Jaipur and the Netherlands

ISBN: 81-7436-289-4
Rs. 295

Typeset in Minion by Roli Books Pvt. Ltd. and
printed at Tan Prints (India) Pvt. Ltd., Jhajjar, Haryana

To

JAYASHREE
who inspired me to write this memoir
and to my grandchildren

Contents

Acknowledgements

I am thankful to:

Late Professor Jaidev of the English Department of Himachal
Pradesh University, who typed the first draft of my book and
declared it would be a best-seller one day;

Latha Anantharaman for patiently reading the draft—a labour
of love;

Vijaya, my daughter, for patting it into shape with her
magical touch;

Krish, my son-in-law, for doing everything to make the
manuscript print worthy;

Indira Menon for introducing me to Roli Books;

Namita Gokhale for liking the manuscript;

Pramod Kapoor of Roli Books for publishing the book;

Jitendra Pant, my charming young editor, for making me feel
like an honoured member of the Roli family.

Foreword

W^{ith} the coming of Post-Modernism the era of the mega-narratives has ended. The little narratives of the many have become more significant in reconstructing a period. To put it slightly differently, the de-construction of established historical myths becomes possible only when one views history from below. Elise Boulding, the Canadian feminist, uses an interesting phrase for this genre of writing: The Underside of History. Subaltern writing was a major step in this direction since it moved the headlights on the stage away from the 'heroic' figures and focused on the periphery. Thereby, the marginalized subaltern was brought centrestage. Perhaps one of the problems with the subaltern school was that merely shifting the focus did not alter the essential perception of the relationship as one of subalternism versus domination. Narratives of individuals, diaries of unknown men and women become important in their own right without falling into the paradigmatic trap of subaltern studies.

The present autobiography by Sethu Ramaswamy is one such work, its importance stemming from the fact that it is written by an ordinary housewife. It is not the narration of a Sarojini Naidu or a Kamladevi Chattopadhyaya who, despite their marginalization in gender terms, were nevertheless very much a part of the mega-narrative of those eventful years of the twentieth century as players and participants. Sethu, however, views her life and times through the prism of the commonplace and the commonsensical. Increasingly these are the narratives that people are going to pick up to understand better the various strands that constitute our social and cultural past.

Ramachandra Guha, freelance writer and historian, used a suggestive argument in his article on biography / autobiography writing published in the *Times Literary Review*. Most biographies which are of icons (whether political, social or cultural) tend to become hagiographical and most autobiographies written by public figures underplay the place of the marginal and the ordinary. It is really the lives of 'the people of the middle' which become crucial for a critical understanding of historical events. In this context one would wish to point out that virtually every social historian working on medieval India is turning to the *Ardhakathanak,* the autobiography of a petty Jain merchant, to understand the sociocultural nuances of the medieval world of politics and commerce in northern India.

Sethu's narrative spans seventy years. Her childhood in Kandy in Ceylon (modern Sri Lanka) provides insights into plantation life and slave labour. Children barely out of the lisping stage were sold for a song into slavery; her father's peon Banda also owned a slave. Nor was it uncommon for the poor to send their girls to 'white' sahebs who 'took good care of them and provided for the family'. What the young child's mind recorded then, Sethu puts down with her own self-reflections. Her father's official position as the go-between for the government and the plantation workers enables her to see something of the early Indian labour migration into Ceylon

which today has become a Frankenstein's monster. The life in
Ceylon ends with Sethu's marriage to her cousin Ramaswamy.

The Trivandrum years record a way of life that has virtually
gone—the joint family system. Sethu records superstitions and
fears, the driving away of the evil spirits and the developing of
the *chumai thangi*, a unique custom to honour the memory of
a woman who has died in childbirth. Pre-natal mortality rates
were high and women like Sarojem, Sethu's sister-in-law, died
because of the absence of lady doctors and inadequate medical
aid. Delivery was invariably done by the *dai*. Sethu herself bore
six children and went through a few abortions, and women who
are looking at the social history of Indian medicine, particularly
from a gender perspective, will find much in these pages that
is of interest.

The movement from Trivandrum to New Delhi in 1943 is a
movement from tradition to modernity, to put it simplistically.
Sethu and Ramaswamy were caught in the hub of Independence
politics—Quit India Movement, Gandhi's prayer meetings and
Congress politics. These were also the war years. World War II
for Sethu was a distant happening but it impacted her everyday
housekeeping in unforgettable ways. Women were given two
saris annually on their ration card, and rice on the ration card
was so meagre that it was reserved for the men of the household.
Women waited with bated breath for their husbands to leave
some rice so that they could savour the taste of something which
had become for them a rarity! While every history book of this
era places Gandhi, Nehru and others in the centre of happenings,
Sethu's life is firmly centred around her husband and her
growing family. Gandhi's assassination and the Partition riots
come through poignantly as they shatter the peace of her little
world. For instance, Ramaswamy fled riot-hit Daryaganj with
his eight months pregnant wife Sethu. She delivered her third
daughter, Jayashree, in the safety of the home of a bare
acquaintance on the condition that the couple would leave
within a month after the delivery.

There were six daughters growing up at home and Mr Ramaswamy had returned to journalism after the Chamber of Princes, where he had been serving as Deputy Secretary, folded up in 1947. The pleasures and pains of bringing up a large family on an uncertain income (journalists in those days were paid a pittance) combines with their interaction with the world of politics and politicians. Kashmiri pundits, Ceylonese refugees and the nitty-gritty of the transfer of power get reflected in unexpected ways in Sethu's narrative. Sometimes naïve, at times surprisingly perceptive, Sethu combines her reflections of the personal and political charmingly to cut and paste, mix and match her impressions of those eventful years.

Memory seldom progresses in a linear fashion. It always zigzags from the present to the past and back again in its own quirky fashion. Sethu's narrative makes no effort to order one's memory in an arbitrary manner, but allows it to meander its way back and forth between those seventy years.

I would like to conclude by pointing to the thirst for education that constantly surfaces through Sethu's narrative: her frustrations at being denied the opportunity to study, her secret quest for knowledge which made her learn multiple languages on her own. Her conclusion, in fact, marks the beginning of a new chapter in her life. Sethu, at the age of seventy-nine acquired a master's degree in History from Annamalai University, definitely a record for someone who abandoned school when she was ten to enter into marriage and motherhood. As she says, 'Many old people may have got degrees late in their lives but I have made a quantum leap from kindergarten to post-graduation.'

VIJAYA RAMASWAMY

Preface

❧❧❧

When my husband passed away on 26 May 1992, my world crumbled around me. I had lost a companion of fifty-seven years, my cousin, my husband, my lover and the father of my children. There were great moments and sad moments in our life. There were sunny days when we were radiant and stormy days when we quarrelled. But it was a life lived and shared together. On the credit side we had six loving daughters and had together celebrated the marriages of five, resulting in four grandsons and seven granddaughters.

My husband, despite a hectic journalistic career, lived for his children and spent a lot of time in their company. In a way he was closer to them than I was. He would even advise them about home remedies for a clear skin and for hair care; he helped me in bathing them and braiding their hair. He played with them, read with them, was severe when correcting them and gave them a good sense of values. He was a wonderful father. When we left our residence in Bharati Nagar, New Delhi, for my youngest daughter's flat in Mayur Vihar, we left behind memories of a lifetime. The links snapped.

My youngest daughter Vijaya and I left for Shimla on August 31—at which time I begin writing this memoir. Just before we left, my third daughter, Jayashree, had begged me to write something, anything, even if it were only my thoughts. With her words ringing in my ears and to pass my lonely hours in Shimla, I started writing. My recollections, up to the time my children grew up to be old enough to store their own memories, have been recorded here, so that future generations learn something of the lives and times of their ancestors.

SETHU RAMASWAMY
Shimla, September 1992

'My body lies upon the grass
Peaceful odours of the wood
And dreams of my people filter past,
Images of when I was a child
My father, My mother,
A smile present!'

The Song of Rita Joe

By Way Of Beginning

I began writing these pages from memory, intending to enlighten my children and grandchildren about their ancestors and the times in which they lived. As I wrote I found myself recording not only my family history but the customs, rituals, family structure, and even the ridiculous economics of that time—even half a cent had value. It gradually struck me that perhaps my narrative would interest a larger circle of readers as well.

The shock and grief at the loss of my husband was still raw, and as I sat down to write, memories of the early years of my life mingled with the aching emptiness of the present. Writing a memoir without notes or a diary to refresh one's memory is not easy. But I found that once my mind delved into the past, going as far back as seventy years, I was able to locate myself in those times and surroundings, among people long gone, whose memory the years could not erase. I relived my childhood, skipped into girlhood and saw myself mature into a woman.

This memoir is in three parts. The first part is about my childhood and early years in Kandy, where I grew up and went to school. I lived in Ceylon, now Sri Lanka, at a time when there was no divide between the Tamils and the Sinhalese. The Tamils had a say in the government and there was goodwill and understanding. If one were to research the umbilical ties of India and Ceylon, one could understand the anguish of the Tamils who were claiming their rights in their adopted motherland and also sympathize with the Sinhalese for wanting to establish an identity of their own. The ethnic ties between India and Ceylon have always been there, but the inner tensions and conflicts were slowly surfacing. I have attempted to give a background to the relationship and how India stood vis-à-vis Ceylon, because I belong to both these countries, both these worlds.

I grew up in Kandy where my father worked as an Assistant Agent in the Office of the Government of India. It was his job to look after the interests of the estate labourers. After Ceylon's independence, my father's last posting was as Second Secretary in the Indian High Commission at Colombo. My first child was born in Kandy.

Having taken seriously suggestions from friends and family members who read the manuscript, I have in this brief prologue outlined a historical and political sketch, situating those times for the readers. My only knowledge of history is the history of Ceylon, which I had to study at school. Therefore, whatever history I might write is the history I perceived as a child and understood later through the casual guidance of my husband.

The second part of this book is about my marriage and life in my in-law's house, where I went at the age of thirteen. My in-laws lived in Trivandrum, also my birthplace. Since my father had left for Ceylon to join the office at Kandy, my mother who was expecting me stayed with her brother, my Krishna *mama*, for the delivery. I was born on 24 September 1924 and was named Sethu, meaning 'bridge' in

Sanskrit, as my father had crossed the Sethu to go to Ceylon that very year.

Trivandrum, the capital of Travancore, is a very important city in Kerala. For four generations, beginning with my grandfather, men from my family had been in the service of the Travancore palace. An illustrious ancestor of mine was the great warrior Prime Minister Rama Iyer Dalawa, one of the architects of the many reforms in Travancore State. He also consolidated the kingdom, bringing the petty, warring rajas under the rule of Maharaja Marthanda Varma of Travancore. My grandfather, a Deputy Director of Education in the State, left behind some notes on Rama Iyer Dalawa and the part he played in helping the Maharaja fight his enemies. I have used these in my narrative.

The final phase of this book is set in New Delhi, where I lived with my husband and family for fifty years and continue to live. I came to New Delhi in 1943. My eldest daughter Manju was three years old. It was wartime, with the scarcities that war entailed. It is not for me to write the political history of those times; I have drawn my narrative from personal knowledge of the way the war hit ordinary families like mine.

My writing is more like a travelogue of thoughts. I would be lost in the past and then, suddenly, find myself taking a leap into the present. Occasionally, I found myself weeping or laughing, as I recalled long-forgotten events. Seventy years is a very long period, and the world was very different in the twenties. Two great wars had been fought involving all the major countries of the world; there was a revolution in China and it became a 'People's Republic.'

Despite such world-shaking events terrorism and violence had not become household words. Fiery patriots did oppose Mahatma Gandhi's peaceful methods to attain independence, but they eventually came around to his way of thinking. Gandhi's bloodless struggle, *Satyagraha*, had shown people that by peaceful mass protests, they could wield immense power in their hands. Unfortunately, non-violence is no longer relevant, and in post-independent India states like Kashmir and Punjab have gone through violent upheavals.

My husband came to Delhi in 1942, and I joined him in 1943. We were in Delhi during the pre- and post-Partition riots. In the wake of Partition, during the transition from colonial bondage to freedom, both India and Pakistan went through a horrifying period of mass killings and looting. India may have won independence from the British through non-violent means, but the price for Partition was paid in blood on both sides of the border.

My husband became a journalist during the war years and specialized as a Political Correspondent. Life with him was exciting. I learnt to understand politics, analyze political situations, and assess politicians. Our house was the meeting place for fellow journalists and Members of Parliament from South India. My husband helped them write their political speeches and frame queries for Question Hour in Parliament. Ever since my husband began working as a special correspondent for the *Lake House Papers*, Sri Lanka, Ceylonese officials from the High Commission became frequent visitors to our home.

This narrative is just the story of my life; it is nothing spectacular or great worth recording. It is the saga of a woman who has lived in two countries and seen her own family make the transition from tradition to modernity. In Trivandrum, I lived in a traditional family conforming to the orthodoxy of those times while my later years have been spent in New Delhi, the hub of politics and fashion. Now into the twenty-first century, I feel my life turning a cartwheel.

I

KANDY

Early Recollections

❧❀☙

My first recollection finds me a three-year-old, sitting in a baby cane chair, on the doorstep outside the front room facing the street, cuddling a doll. The doll was not a cuddly one by any means. It was, if I remember clearly, a stiff plastic policeman doll. I was already attending school and had won the doll in a race on sports day.

I can see myself sitting in that chair, babbling to myself. My hair was bobbed close. I was thin, not fair, not dark, but wheatish. I remember myself as a quiet, playful kid. Why this scene should stick in my mind seventy years later, I fail to fathom.

We lived in a house at Peradeniya Road in Kandy for three years and then moved into a better accommodation further up the street. Both my elder sisters Krishna and Goma were in the Kandy house with my parents. My younger sister Padma, or Padha as we call her, was born two years later, after we moved to the bigger house. Daddy was a very fair and

handsome man, but he was short. He was only five feet five
inches tall and was respectfully known as *Rao Bahadur* A.S.
Narayanan. After Independence when he settled down in Salem,
he dropped the title and was popularly referred to as 'Ceylon'
Narayanan Iyer. My mother was slim and good-looking though
dark. My mother's name was Anandammal and even her
grandchildren called her by that name. Daddy told us, years
later, the story of how and when their marriage was fixed.

Daddy was eleven and Mother eight and a half. He saw the
bride and refused to marry her, because of her complexion.
His mother gave him a tight slap saying, 'How dare you refuse
to marry Chamy's daughter?' Chamy was short for
Ramaswamy, my maternal grandfather who was a cousin of
my paternal grandmother. The premarital negotiations were like
a classic movie scene in which the bridegrooms are switched.
My grandfather had settled my mother's marriage with a boy
called Ramakrishnan, whose father owned lands and property
and was considered wealthy. For his brother's daughter he had
fixed up A.S. Narayanan, my father, who belonged to a large
family consisting of eight sisters and two brothers. Since my
father was a good student my grandfather had hopes of
educating his future son-in-law and getting him a good job, as
he felt responsible for his late brother's family.

Society was strictly patriarchal then and the head of the
family had the final say in all matters. My grandfather was a
big man both in stature and status, and the family stood in
awe of him. But, a household member demurred about the
marriage. Grandfather overheard his sister-in-law complaining
that since she was a dependent, her daughter Chellam was to
be given in marriage to a boy with eight sisters, (whose
marriages would be the boy's responsibility), while for
Grandfather's own daughter her brother-in-law had fixed
up a boy with land and property. Hearing her unjust words,
my grandfather immediately switched bridegrooms. A.S.
Narayanan married my mother, prospered, and won honours,

eventually acquiring the title of *Rao Bahadur*, while Mr Ramakrishnan lost all his property and poor Chellam lived a life of penury.

The first house we lived in had a living room and two bedrooms in the front. There was a courtyard and beyond that was the kitchen. We had our meals in the kitchen, sitting on the floor. I remember once, when it had been raining for days without end, the open passage that led to the kitchen was flooded and water got into the kitchen as well. We had to wade through knee-deep water to wash our hands and the plates. I thought it great fun and was splashing about trying to do a few breast strokes, when I was hauled out and my ears boxed. There were many other rainy days and many other watery episodes, but this is the only one that I remember, perhaps because of the cuffing I received!

I was not a mischievous or troublesome child. My favourite game was to line up all the chairs in the house and play at being teacher, tutoring all the invisible pupils. I had started going to school with my sisters when I was barely three years old. Most middle- and upper-class children in Ceylon went to mission schools. The teachers of the lower KG (there was no nursery class then) refused to take me as I was underage. I would create a scene every morning when my sisters Krishna and Goma left for school and cried so much to be taken with them that Daddy went to the school and spoke to the Principal. I gained admission as a special case.

I was a precocious child and very soon was much ahead of the others in class. My teacher, Miss Orloff, used to ask me to read out to the class from the primer called *Songs the Letters Sing* or make them recite nursery rhymes while she went out of the classroom—probably for a relaxed chat in the staff room. I suppose that is how I came to teach empty chairs at home, frequently admonishing children to keep a 'finger on your lips.' That was seventy years ago and now I see my little granddaughter, Medha, playing the same game.

I invariably made my elder sisters late for school. They would wait for me to get ready, but sometimes went off leaving me behind. On such days, Daddy's office peon Ramanarayanan, a Tamilian, would carry me all the way to school. I wonder now if my dilly-dallying was not deliberate. But, no! I was not a clever child in that sense. I was always thought of by others to be a simpleton, and being the youngest, I was spoilt a great deal.

A frightening incident occurred at our old house on the day of the festival of *Perehera*, the Tooth Festival which falls in August. A big fair was held in Kandy town, and our peon Ramanarayanan was commissioned to take me to the fair. There were giant Catherine wheels, swings, merry-go-rounds, magic shows, lucky dips and the usual eatery stalls. I do not remember much of what I did, but do remember winning a tiny cup and saucer in a lucky dip, buying ribbons, and some fancy things. We left the fair in time to reach home to see the procession, which would have started from the *Dalada Maligawa*, the temple of the Lord Buddha, and would be passing through our street. Anantha, Krishna and Goma—my memory is vague about this point—must have been at home. I can only ask Goma; Anantha and Krishna are no more. It was night when the grand procession came to our street. I was thrilled to see elephants; there were baby elephants, elephants of all heights, there were elephants galore. The huge ones carried the decorated palanquins of Kandyan kings, ordinary men dressed up in costumes, and also Kandyan chieftains with big bellies, wearing red cummerbunds and gorgeous turbans. Why they had such big bellies I could not for the life of me understand. There were the Kandyan dancers, beating the drums and dancing, and people wearing masks of lions and tigers and acrobats performing.

On the day of the festival, Daddy and Mama had gone out for a ride on the motor bike. I vividly remember them coming back late in the night and saw that Mama's sari was torn and her hand and face were bleeding. It seems that the sari had got stuck in the wheel and while trying to remove the sari she had hurt her hand, too. The house was dark and as she came in, she heard utensils clattering in the backyard. Mama at once grabbed a lamp in her hand and went straight down to the kitchen shouting boldly, 'Who is there?' A thief. As soon as he heard Mama's voice, he dropped his bundle and ran away through the back door. Mama bolted the door, looked around and found a bundle containing the vessels. I was so frightened that I clung to Mama's sari and cried. When Daddy came back after parking the motorcycle, he went around the house to see if the thief was lurking around. I have never forgotten that day. I remember thinking then that my mother was brave and courageous and she has always been so.

It was in the old house that Daddy's cousin, Judge Subbaiyer, came to visit us. He was a fair, stout man. He wore diamond studs in his ears and a gold lace turban. He was reputed to be mean and stingy. If he was travelling with his family on a train and it halted at railway stations where peddlers blew toy whistles and shook rattles to attract children, Judge Sahib would talk loudly so that the toy-sellers' noise would be drowned. Thus the clever man saved the expense of a few annas! Being a judge and a high dignitary, he had an authoritative manner. He would call the peons *Adai,* a term used in addressing urchins—so the peons used to refer to him as 'Adai Swami.' We were all relieved when his visit came to an end.

I remember the house we moved into next. We called it the Ghafoor House after the Muslim landlord. This house had one floor and it was nearer to school by two furlongs, as we had moved up the street. My sisters Padma and Sarasa were born there in 1929 and 1932 respectively.

We all slept upstairs. The wooden flooring allowed us to peer down and see what was going on downstairs. We had a cowshed at the back of the house, with a cow and two calves. As long as we were in Kandy we used to have our own cows for our daily milk. The cows were big Australian breeds yielding as much as 10 to 15 litres of milk. Sometimes in the night we would hear the cow mooing loudly. Daddy would call out to Anantha to go down to the cowshed and feed the cow with hay or grass. Anantha was a coward and would call Krishna to come with him. She would pull her blanket tightly over her face and flatly refuse. Anantha would plead and plead with her, perhaps promising her some reward in return. Grumbling, she would get up and go with him.

The eldest in the family, my brother Anantha, comes to my mind when I think of Ghafoor house, where we lived for three years. I can't remember him before that. He went to Kingswood College, a boy's school and a brother organization of our school, the Kandy Methodist Girls High School. He finished his schooling there and was sent to Trivandrum for further studies. His subject was mathematics. He was brilliant, but boisterous beyond compare, and quite a prankster. He and Krishna were the only ones to get corporal punishment from Daddy, who at times even used his belt.

As a child I was a sleepwalker. I would get up at night and in my sleep, change my dress, sit in front of the mirror to comb my hair, put on my shoes and go downstairs. The front door was bolted from the top, so I could not reach it. Since everyone knew of my habit, they were alert. My sisters, who slept in the room with me, would wake up, follow me downstairs, and carry me back to bed. Daddy had a carpenter come in to fix a door over the top of the stairs. At night this door would be locked. As I grew up, I mercifully got over the habit.

Kandy town was a mile or two away from Peradeniya Road. We used to go there for shopping or just for a walk. Once Daddy took me and me alone to town, to a toyshop. The name of the shop was Marikkar Stores. Daddy was in a generous mood and asked me to take anything I liked from the shop. I see myself, a tiny skinny child of four, looking around the shop and picking a huge celluloid doll. It was so big I couldn't carry it. Daddy was amused and gladly paid the price of Rs 5 for it. I came home bubbling with joy. I still have the doll with me.

I brought it away from Kandy when we left Ceylon forever and it has been with me these seventy-one years. There are many photographs in our family album showing Padha and Sarasa with the doll. Now my grandchildren hug the huge doll to their chests and play with it.

I was in the Second Standard and perhaps seven years old at that time. Sarasa and Padha were not old enough for school. I was to take part in a gypsy dance in the school concert. We had to wear a costume. Mama made mine at home: a red skirt of taffeta silk with a blouse and a sash, and a multi-coloured scarf to tie on my head. We were told by our teacher to wear as many bangles as we could get hold of. My sister Goma was always a steady and serious-minded girl. Her trunk was full of treasures, coloured ribbons carefully packed in a box, fancy hair slides, hair clips, and various other items. Among her collection she had a box full of beautiful glass bangles from India. As soon as bangles were mentioned my mind flew to Goma's treasure box, but I was scared to ask her. Just the day before the concert my ensemble was complete, except for the bangles. I went to Goma and asked her meekly and humbly if she could spare a few pairs of bangles just for the concert and promised that I would be careful not to break them and would return them safely. She flatly refused, not without cause, as I was a careless and playful child and could not be trusted with anything valuable. I pleaded and wept; she didn't relent. Mama saw me in this pitiable state and took up my cause. She told Goma, 'Why don't you give that poor child a few bangles? She only wants them for the concert and promises to bring them back safely.' After much persuasion and strong words from Mama, Goma reluctantly gave me five or six pairs. They had golden stars shining on the coloured glass and were really beautiful. I took them in a box to school on the day of the concert.

I had a classmate Inez, who was snooty and not friendly to me. She was a well-built girl and had a lot of clout with our class teacher, who was her aunt. Inez was bowled over when she saw the bangles and became sweet and friendly. I was so happy and flattered to be noticed by such an important girl, silly goose that I was! I promised to give her just one pair after the concert. She was grateful and put her arm through mine to show everyone she was my friend. After the concert she came to claim her pair. Along with her were other girls who were all praising me and my bangles. It went to my head and I parted with a few more pairs. By then it was time to go home. Daddy had come to pick me up. I came home with an empty box. Goma would have killed me if she could, if she had caught me alone, but I studiously avoided her and stayed near Daddy and Mama. She cried and cried for her bangles. Looking back, I wonder why she didn't strangle me, I deserved it. Even today I feel ashamed when I think of having been such a stupid fool!

We soon shifted from Ghafoor House, this time just four or five houses down the street. One Mr Paulraj and his wife used to occupy that house, and we used to visit them. They were a young couple. Mrs Paulraj used to come to Mama for advice on any problem she had. We moved in after they left. We liked the house, but we liked the house next door much more. One of the windows of our house opened out on the garden of the next house. All of us used to gaze at the lovely garden and front porch and dream of living in that house.

That dream came true and we moved next door to Arifa House. It was named after one of the daughters of the landlord Mr Ismail. Arifa House, 321 Peradeniya Road, is an address I can never forget. It was a beautiful colonial house with a front porch and a few steps leading to a large three-sided verandah. The front portion of the house had a huge drawing room and a dining room with one guest room on the left and three huge bedrooms in a row on the right. The kitchen and pantry were at a lower level, with steps leading from the back verandah. We had a spacious garden at the front and a lot of ground at the back. The cow shed at the back had two Australian cows and two or three calves. We later sold off the male calves.

Our home was on high ground and one could see the main railway line down below through which all the important trains passed by. The train from Talaimannar went up to Colombo, and passengers from India coming to Kandy had to get down at Kadugannava and take the train to Kandy. My eldest brother-in-law, Pamanji Anna, would come to visit us from Salem, a district near Chennai, and we would wait for his train to pass through. He would throw small gift parcels for us from the train, and we would be thrilled to pick them up and climb up the slope to our home hugging our treasures. My brother Anantha would also come by that train on his annual holidays, but he never brought us any gifts as he was always impoverished and badly in need of money. I remember the only letters he wrote from Trivandrum were on post cards and they always began, 'Dear Papa, I am well and hope the same there. Can you please send me Rs 50 as soon as possible? I need the money urgently. With *namaskarams* to you and Mama, yours affectionately . . .'

In those days in Ceylon, a kind of slavery was in practice. Little girls and boys were bought from poor people and made to work as servants in the house. They were mostly children ranging from eight to twelve years of age. Mrs Paulraj had a little servant girl. She had to do all the work in the house, and was not paid for it, as she had been bought.

I remember seeing her having tea and bread after serving hoppers, a delicious Ceylonese preparation, with tea and eggs to the family. She would sit or rather squat on the floor with a little salt in her left hand and her teacup in her right. She would take a sip or two of tea—without milk of course—and lick the salt from her left hand. Her breakfast would be a few slices of stale bread. The first time I saw her I was shocked. A thin underfed waif, her hair was cropped close to keep it clean and she wore a jacket and sarong, the Sinhalese dress. Many houses had this slave system. Even Daddy's peon Banda, a Sinhalese, had bought a girl to work for his family. He himself had five children.

Ramanarayanan, Banda and another Tamil named Suppiah were the three peons under Daddy. We had other servants, of course. I remember Mary, an ayah, and Krishnan, a Brahmin cook. When we were in Ghafoor House there was a Tamil woman, Chellamma, working for us. She had quite a brood. Her youngest son Chinnathambi was an urchin of two or three years. He would cry and stamp his feet alternately. I would get so irritated that I felt like slapping him. Chellamma had a fairly good-looking daughter of about fifteen or sixteen.

Chellamma once narrated this story to Mama. It seems a European estate owner wanted a girl and the procuring agent disclosed this to Chellamma, saying that her daughter would be paid well and given new clothes and jewellery. Chellamma, who lived in abject poverty, sent this girl to the tea-estate planter. She was telling Mama how good the *Dorai* was. I was too young to understand but I heard the story, and later connected it to the iniquities and atrocities committed by European planters. As I grew up I came to realize that the plight of Chellamma's daughter was shared by many poor Tamil girls. The girls were abandoned by their white protectors when they grew tired of them, leaving behind children who were colloquially called *Chi-Chis*, children who found acceptance in neither community. This fate was shared by the colonized poor in other countries as well and the Mulattoes of America faced social ostracism similar to the Ceylonese and Indian *Chi-Chis*.

My memories of Kandy remain vivid. It was a charming town surrounded by lush, green hills, which made the landscape breathtakingly beautiful. A splash of colour greeted you whichever way you looked as the hills rose on the horizon. The small chic bungalows with red roofs and smooth macadamized roads relieved with parks and gardens made Kandy almost a garden city.

Kandy was generally cool, with light showers throughout the year. We did not have ceiling fans in the house, but even in the early thirties, the sewage system was good and septic tanks were installed. Kandy was the capital of the Sinhalese kings, chosen for its strategic location, as it was a valley hidden by surrounding hills, making it a natural fort. As in most historical betrayals, the last king of Ceylon was deceived by one of his own trusted chiefs to the British.

During World War II, Kandy came into the world map when Lord Mountbatten, who had an eye for grandeur and beauty as well as military genius, chose the little known township tucked away in the Sri Lankan hills to establish his South East area command. But the importance of Kandy to the local people stemmed from the famous *Dalada Maligawa,* the Temple of the Tooth, and the *Perehera.*

Sri Lanka's history has been both fascinating and tantalizing. There is an umbilical cord which binds India and Sri Lanka and is seen in geographical proximity, crosscurrents of culture, religion, politics and ethnic ties. Continuous contacts and conflicts have, over the course of centuries, built a love-hate relationship between India and Sri Lanka. For centuries the Sinhalese kings had to combat periodical invasions from the Chola and Pandyan kings of South India. The ambivalent relationship between the two countries and the Tamils of India and Sri Lanka is tellingly illustrated in Nilakanta Shastri's classic textbook, *A History of South India.* Narasimhavarman, the Pallava king, led a naval expedition to Ceylon to help King Manavarman in the internal civil war, while Varaguna Pandya ransacked Sri Lanka, especially Anuradhapura, in A.D. 830. This ambivalence continued in the case of the imperial Cholas as well. It is said that in A.D. 1084, Vijayabahu of Ceylon declared war on the Cholas when he heard that the envoys he had sent to the court of Vikramaditya VI had been mutilated. While Vijayabahu was preparing for the expedition, the Tamil *velaikkara,* or soldiers, 'unwilling to fight their Tamil kinsmen, mutinied, and burnt the royal palace'. This incident is recorded in an inscription at Polonnaruva in Ceylon. It is the umbilical cord which binds the Tamils in both lands that perhaps accounts for the Sri Lankan fear of India, the belligerent Big Brother.

The strongest link between India and Sri Lanka has been Buddhism. Two thousand and five hundred years ago, a sacred link was established between the two countries through it. This story is remembered in both countries with considerable nostalgia: how the Mauryan Emperor Ashoka sent his son Mahendra and daughter Sanghamitra to an unknown land across the seas with a Bo sapling from Bodh Gaya. We read about Buddhism coming from India to Sri Lanka in our school textbooks. The mission of the children of the emperor was to spread the message of *ahimsa* (non-violence) and *karuna* (compassion), which Lord Buddha had taught Ashoka. The message of the Buddha had turned the king from the path of war and destruction to the path of peace and righteousness. Buddhists from Sri Lanka still come to Nepal on a pilgrimage to Lumbini, the birthplace of Lord Buddha; to Bodh Gaya, where he attained enlightenment; and to Sarnath where he gave his first discourse about the *dharma chakra parivartana*. There are numerous other sites in India associated with the Buddha's sacred relics.

My father was an Assistant Agent, working with Mr K.P.S. Menon, the Agent at the Government of India Office in Ampitiya. The place was just five or six miles from Peradeniya Road. The Agent's bungalow, a large sprawling house with huge lawns and gardens surrounding it, was on a hill. The office was at a lower level. Two or three miles from it was Kadugastota, where a small river flowed. Mahouts would bring herds of elephants to the river for bathing. Daddy used to take us there, and I had great fun watching the elephants play, blowing water from their trunks and spraying fountains of water at each other.

The purpose of the India Office in Kandy was to look after the large labour population in the tea and rubber estates. Daddy had to go round the tea estates and see to the welfare of the Indian labourers. He toured the length and breadth of Ceylon, wherever there were tea estates. He did a great deal for the coolies, as the Indian labourers were called. There used to be a *Kangani,* or headman, over the coolies, then an overseer. Above the overseer was the superintendent, usually a white man; then came the English planter. There were other categories, mostly occupied by Sinhalese or Dutch burghers, who were clerks and officers. The *Kangani* was usually a Tamil to facilitate dealing with the coolies in Tamil.

Sometimes Daddy would take Mama and us on his tours of the tea estates. Much before entering the estate one could breathe the exhilarating aroma of fresh tea. That flavour and the tea estates come to my mind whenever I think of Ceylon as do the beautiful greenish grey hills in 'up-country' plantation territory.

These pleasant memories are mixed with the painfully sad images of the coolies. I have seen the coolies' rows of miserable huts with patched up leaky tin roofs, where the Indian labourers lived. They were without exception exploited and underpaid. Since they had to go early to the tea plantations and pluck the leaves, the coolies were given their afternoon gruel, which consisted of watery rice and salt. Women and children mostly did the plucking; the men had heavier work to do. I used to watch the women plucking the tea leaves with baskets tied behind them. They were experts in separating the buds from the tender leaves. Sometimes they strapped their very young babies to their backs. Generations of these coolies lived, raised children, and died in these miserable conditions with no hope for the future. I don't know what they were paid—perhaps only 10 or 15 cents a basket (1 Ceylonese Rupee = 100 cents). I cannot be accurate. There were also rubber estates in Ceylon, where coolies were employed for tapping the milk from rubber trees. The miserable condition of the Tamil estate labourers was the theme of a poem by the great Tamil poet, patriot, and visionary, Subramanya Bharati. It was titled *Teyilai Thottathile* meaning *In the Tea Plantations.* The famous Carnatic musician

Musiri Subramanya Iyer rendered the song on a gramophone record. The song moved many people to tears.

I heard about the coolie strikes and protests when their conditions deteriorated. The labourers' relations with the plantation supervisors turned sour and the situation became tense. Daddy intervened: he talked to the superintendent, pacified the coolies, listened to their woes and took up their grievances with the plantation owners to ensure these were redressed. My father did a lot to improve the working condition of the coolies and was awarded the title of *Rao Sahib* in recognition of his role as mediator.

The Indian plantation labourers constituted the largest group among people of Indian origin. The Diaspora Indians also sustained themselves in various kinds of employment, apart from being successful in business and manufacturing. There were prosperous merchants from the Sindhi and Bohra Muslim communities, hailing originally from Bombay (now Mumbai). The Chettiars from the Tamil country, who are equivalent to the Banias, were another important group of merchants. The Jaffna Tamils, whether they belonged to the northern or eastern province, identified themselves more with the Sinhalese than with the Indian Tamils. However, during the last two decades they have been drifting away from the Sinhalese and making common cause with the Indian Tamils. The Northern and Eastern provinces, where the Tamils dominate, are now strife-torn areas with the Liberation Tigers for Tamil Eelam (LTTE) waging a war for freedom from Sinhalese governance. But, all this is recent history.

In the past, Anantha, my brother was studying in the Arts College, Trivandrum. My eldest sister Krishna was married to Ananthakrishnan, the son of Aunt Chellamma, Daddy's eldest sister. This was probably in 1928 or 1929. Ananthakrishnan's pet name was Pamanji and we called him Pamanji Anna.

I was studying in the Third Standard. I liked school and was considered a good student. But I was indifferent about my dress and careless about my books. I remember losing all my books once after I had rid myself of my school bag in a corner of the playground. When it was time to go home, I looked for my bag and found it, but a lot of books were missing. I managed that whole term without books, trusting to my memory by reading from my friends' books after school hours.

My favourite games were hopscotch, catch and run, and a game called rounders. Played with a tennis ball, rounders is somewhat like baseball. We also played net ball, now called basketball. Playing catch and run was great fun. We had a nonsensical doggerel to select the person who would be the catcher. Whoever the last word of the doggerel fell on was eliminated. The girl who remained at the end was the catcher and the others were the runners. The doggerel went like this:

Eena Meena Dyna do,
Cattle weena wyna wo,
Eace peace must be done,
Illian, Tillian Twenty-one.

Another doggerel read:

One, two, three, four, five, six, seven
All good children go to heaven
Where their sins are all forgiven
One, two, three, four, five, six, seven.

We played the game with deadly seriousness.

Our school started at 8 a.m. So in the morning we only had time for some bread and tea or milk. In the afternoon, Mama used to send our lunch through one of the peons. The way lunch was brought in Kandy was different from the way food is packed here. It was not packed in a lunch box; the rice and vegetables and curry were heaped on one plate and covered with another plate. This was tied in a napkin and the fork and spoon were tucked in a loop in the napkin. Sometimes Mama used to send the food in a tiffin carrier and it was kept in a house opposite the school. Daddy's office clerk Mr Raghuraman lived there. We used to go to his house to have our lunch.

Miss White was my teacher in the Second Standard. She took scripture lessons during Bible class. I liked the lessons, was good in answering questions, and scored good marks in the subject. Miss White was something of a missionary; she would say that those who were not Christians were heathens, and she tried to convert me. I just did not like that and made it clear to her that I did not like it. But those scripture lessons made a deep impression on me and I love Jesus Christ. I used to join the groups singing Christmas carols on Christmas Eve. Miss Nelson, Inez's aunt, taught me in the Fourth Standard. She had married a member of Daddy's staff, Mr Kymal, a Malayali Muslim. I hated her and was unhappy in her class. Perhaps she took it out on me because Daddy was her husband's boss.

I was an imaginative child and would dream of doing great deeds, somewhat along the lines of Walter Mitty (I saw this movie many years later). In those days every slab of Cadbury's chocolate had a stamp-sized picture of film stars from Hollywood as well as from Bombay inside the outer wrapping. Ceylon did not then have a film industry. Once when I opened a slab of chocolate, I found a picture of a beautiful Indian film star with 'Enakshi Rama Rao' written at the bottom. I took the picture to my school and showed it around to my classmates. There were admiring cries of 'How beautiful she is!' In very modest tones I announced that she was an aunt of mine. To me there was no difference between an Iyer, my sub-caste, and a Rao who may or may not have been a Shaivite and hailed from a different region. She was an Indian, and I decided that she was my aunt. For some days I moved about basking in the importance of being related to a film star. I almost believed it myself.

Wanting to be in the limelight was a trait discernible much earlier, when I was in the Third Standard. I had a friend named Myrtle Fernandes. One day she was absent and the teacher announced that Myrtle's mother had died and the whole class was taken to her house. That was my first encounter with death. The coffin was placed in the centre of the room and all of us went around the coffin and our teacher laid a wreath on it. Myrtle came to school after a week and everyone was kind to her and all the teachers made her sit near them and gave her special attention. Myrtle was certainly my friend, and I was very sorry for her, but I did envy her being the centre of attention. Deep down I was disappointed that someone in my house had not died and enabled me to get all that fuss and attention.

I took Tamil instead of Sinhalese from the first standard. In the Third Standard we had to learn Tamil poetry, *Avvaiyar Cheiyul* and other poems. Being the only Tamil student, I bagged the prize for excellence in Tamil.

In the Fourth Standard, we had a rich girl in our class. She once spent almost all her fee buying guavas and olives for the whole class. The guavas in Kandy are so good that my mouth waters just thinking of them. There were a variety of fruits like *ramutang* and *mangosteen*. *Ramutang* is round and red, the outer skin has tiny hair-like shoots, and the fruit inside is delicious. *Mangosteen* is a purple fruit with a hard thick skin and soft white pulp inside, which was very sweet. Then there were *jumbos*, juicy white and pink fruits to be eaten with the skin. We also had olives, which had a tangy flavour, and a tiny variety of guavas, which was also sweet. I often long to eat those fruits, but it is more than sixty years since I left Kandy and I have not come across these fruits since then. There was also the national sweet of Ceylon—coconut burfi—but made differently from our Indian burfi. These big square pieces of burfi were wrapped in tissue paper and the corners twisted like bon-bon. Just 5 cents for a small piece and 10 for a big piece. Ceylonese food, of course, cannot be described. You have to eat it to know the distinct taste. Since Ceylon is a land of coconuts, most of the Ceylonese dishes are based on coconut milk. They have a breakfast preparation called hoppers, with variants like string hoppers and pittu, all of which are rice and coconut preparations. Ceylon is also famous for its fish. Like the Bengalis, Ceylonese are great fish eaters and have fish everyday. In front of most houses one can see dried fish called *karuvadu*. These can be preserved and fried whenever needed. These fish are just 1' or 2' long.

Our family was strictly vegetarian, and I have never tasted fish except once. Daddy had a clerk named Swaminathan, a Jaffna Tamil. I was a child of six or seven. One day he took me on his motorbike, with Daddy's permission of course, to his house. They gave me lunch there with fish curry. I took a bite of the floating pieces in the curry and got up and said it tasted funny and I didn't like it. They told me it was fish and it was tasty. Why didn't I try to eat a little? I refused and started crying. After some time Uncle Swaminathan brought me back. Another day he took me out and, perhaps he had been drinking, for he started beating me. I do not know for what. I told Daddy and he scolded and shouted at him. After that I never went out with Uncle Swaminathan again.

There was one Krishna Iyer, a Palghat Brahmin, also employed in Daddy's office. They had a daughter about my age or perhaps a little older. I have been to their house; they stayed near the office. She was learning Carnatic music from a *Bhagavathar* (music teacher). After some time, people started saying that the teacher had kept a love letter in the harmonium. The mother found it and that was the end of her music lessons. I believe, after that, in our South Indian Brahmin circles, male music teachers were not very popular.

I was also learning vocal Carnatic music from a music teacher who used to come from Colombo every weekend. All I managed to learn from him were the musical scales taught to beginners. I did not go any further, as he stopped coming.

There was another Head Clerk in Daddy's office, Mr Menon. I came to know later that Daddy did not like him, as he was a cunning man and intrigued against Daddy. We once went to his house, all of us, and we were given coffee in cups. I liked the coffee so much that after coming home I asked Mama to make coffee that way. She burst out laughing and said, 'Why child, they had just poured hot water into a pot which had some coffee powder, and poured it into the cups like tea, added a little milk and a lot of sugar. There was a lot of coffee powder mixed up in the liquid, it was just awful.' Whatever she might say, to me it had tasted wonderful.

Daddy's boss in the office was Mr K.P.S. Menon. After Independence, he became India's Ambassador to China. After the Indo-China war, it was said that three Malayalis—K.P.S. Menon, K.M. Panikkar, and Krishna Menon—were responsible for the 1962 war. They did not read the Chinese signals correctly and advised Nehru wrongly about the 'friendly' intentions of the Chinese, who with the slogan 'Hindi-Chini Bhai Bhai' on their lips attacked our frontiers. The betrayal of Tibet was also largely due to mishandling by our Foreign Office and Defence Ministry.

Sometimes Goma and I used to spend time with the Menons' children. There were two sets of twins other than the two elder girls who also looked like twins. They had funny pet names—Ammani, Kunjan, Ali, Thuli, Manda, and Gudu. Manda is now K.P.S. Menon, Jr. He followed in his father's footsteps and entered the IFS and was posted as India's Ambassador to China. K.P.S. Menon would take us children for long walks up to the cemetery, which was a beautiful place, and while walking he would tell us funny stories and make us laugh. Mrs Saraswati Menon was a beautiful and gracious lady and Mama admired her so much that she named my youngest sister after her.

Going back to my school days, Sports Day was an important function. We started practising for the events a month earlier.

My name was entered for the championship events—the 100 metre, hurdle and relay race. I, still in the first form, was chosen for these events though only seniors from the sixth form participated in them. I was a swift runner and the seniors had nicknamed me Daddy Long Legs. My class teachers made a fuss over me and cautioned me not to fall ill. Wasn't I proud and on top of the world? We were taken to Kingswood College for the 100-metre race. Unfortunately, I did not win any of the championships, but instead came in a poor third. My teachers were not disappointed at my performance, as the third position would entitle me to a prize, and I had competed against girls much older than me. They thought it was a fairly good performance. I know and only I can know why I failed to get better than a third—the elastic in my underwear was loose and I had to hold it, over my frock, so that it would not slip down. I even lost the hurdles because of this. I was a real fool. If only I had asked someone to mend it, I would not have been handicapped. But didn't I mention earlier that I was a scatterbrain!

In our school, as in all public schools, we had a system of houses. Our houses were called Lawrence, Langdon, Eton, and Samson. I was in Samson House. The colours for the four houses were yellow, red, green, and blue. We had to wear our heart-shaped house badges on our uniform, which was a white pleated frock.

On Sports Day, each house was given one corner of the field to pitch their camps in. Each house had a captain. There were huge rolls of matting, and we would take two rolls, open out a length from one roll of matting and roll it around the other roll on the other side, so a portion was cordoned off as our house. We had a big barrel of lemonade free for the members. Coconut burfis were kept on a table, but they were for sale. Almost every Sports Day, I had been a recipient of at least one prize. The third prize in a championship was an honour and there were loud cheers for the lanky kid from the first form as she went on the stage to collect her prize.

So life went on in Kandy, between school and other activities. There were some big girls in my class, perhaps older than me by one or two years and they whispered and giggled together and talked about boys and love. I was severely kept away, perhaps because I was too innocent to be trusted with such secrets. I was awfully sore about it though.

Those were the days when the radio had just come to our part of the world. Daddy came home one day with a big HMV radio set and a technician to get it working. We all crowded round it and were thrilled to hear the Madras station. Whenever there was a Carnatic music programme we would all sit very close to the radio, looking intensely into it, as if trying to catch a glimpse of the singer.

The 1930s and the 1940s were the heydays of M.S. Subbulakshmi, D.K. Pattammal, Chembai Vaidyanatha Bhagavathar, G.N. Balasubramaniam and also the twelve-year-old prodigy Balamurali Krishna. I think he must be around seventy now. Mama used to listen to him and say 'Krishnane avatharam Seithirukkiran (Lord Krishna himself is born).'

Another genius in the limelight was S. Balachandar. As a chess prodigy at ten he had come to play in Ceylon. The whole family was talented. They had all acted in a performance of the Ramayana, and the play was recorded on HMV gramophone discs. The father, mother and the children had all acted in it. Balachandar was a genius, he could do many things, and was also a sitar player. Later, he took to the veena and mastered it.

Visitors from India to Kandy would stay either in the agent's bungalow or with us. Many famous personalities stayed with us. I do not remember many names, but I remember the great freedom fighter S. Satyamurthy, his wife, and his daughter Lakshmi. Daddy used to take the guests to the tea estates and to 'up-country' places like Nuwareliya. On summer holidays our family went to Nuwareliya. It is in the hills, like Ooty in South India. It is cold there, but simply beautiful. All kinds of exotic flowers, which elsewhere have to be carefully cultivated, grow wild on the hills.

One also finds Sita Eliya (*Eliya* means place) there. Legend has it that Sita was imprisoned by the Lankan king Ravana in a forest of Ashoka trees. A dense forest of Ashoka trees is still at Sita Eliya, and the mountain walls are charred like charcoal. Ravana, the *asura* king of Lanka, had brought Sita, the wife of Lord Rama, to his country by force. Hanuman, the king of devotees and beloved of Rama, went to Lanka in search of Goddess Sita. He appeared before Sita just when she had decided to end her life. Hanuman gave her Rama's ring as proof of his own identity and delivered the message that Lord Rama would soon come to Lanka with a huge army to defeat Ravana and rescue his beloved Sita. But, the King of Lanka captured Hanuman and ordered that Hanuman's tail be set on fire. Hanuman with his burning tail set Lanka ablaze, the charred rocks being evidence of his wrath. Near Sita Eliya there is a stream running through the forest with rocks of different shapes that are white in colour with a hint of yellow. They say Sita used to rub turmeric on the rocks and apply it to her face and body while bathing in the stream.

We stayed in the guest house, enjoyed the meals and the walks, and drank in the beauty of the place. We could freely pluck flowers, which grew wild. There were orchids, carnations, chrysanthemums, bar button daisies, sweet williams, lilies, esthers, sweet peas, and fox gloves.

For some holidays, the whole family went to Colombo. We stayed with friends. Once Daddy rented a house for a month in Wellawatte near the beach. But very often we stayed with V.S. Rao and his wife Padma. The Raos were well-off and lived in a spacious house in Wellawatte. They had no children. Mr Rao was a quiet gentleman, but his wife was a character. She was short and plump and had been utterly spoilt by her husband who treated her like a child. She was mad about films and drama and actors. In those days men acted the female roles.

There were theatre groups from India who came to perform in Colombo, and naturally the Indians there put them up as guests in their homes. At least two or three members of the troupe would be accommodated in Mr Rao's house. Padma used to serve them as if they were gods and look at them and sigh and say, 'How lucky your wife is—to be married to an actor like you!' She behaved in such a silly manner that Mama chided her and told her not to behave like a schoolgirl. Mama used to treat her like a younger sister and would take the liberty of scolding her. Whenever she saw us enter the house on a visit with our bags, she would pretend to have a headache and would not get up from bed. Mama used to go to the kitchen, make coffee for all and tell her, 'Enough, Padma, don't sulk, we are going to stay here only for two days, get up.' Then she would say, 'No, *mami*, please stay as long as you like, you know me too well to misunderstand me.'

Whenever the Raos came to Kandy, they—naturally—stayed with us. Padma had another habit of just flicking away little things she liked without so much as a by your leave. It was not kleptomania, but a deliberate habit of taking what she liked. So when we knew they were coming Mama used to put away any fancy item that would catch Padma's eye. But, Padma could always pick on something. Mama had a cute little *vellodu* (bell metal) mug in which she kept milk. Padma eyed it longingly. Mama noticed this and said: 'Padma, you are not to take this mug. If you do I will come to your house and search for it and bring it back. Who knows what else I may find?' She was embarrassed and said, 'No, this is too big for me. I want a smaller one.' And Mama said, 'Yes, I shall get one for you when I go to Trivandrum next.' Mr Rao knew about his wife's weaknesses and secretly appreciated Mama pulling her up, though he never had the courage or the heart to scold her.

Another family I remember was that of Easwaran, the editor of the newspaper *Virakesari*. The Easwarans were Tanjore people. They made excellent coffee served in big tumblers, but the food they cooked for their family of five and for guests was hardly sufficient for two people who ate well. As soon as we went to their house Mama used to call Mrs Easwaran and tell her, 'Look here Lakshmi, you are Tanjore people and do not cook and eat much. But we eat well, so please make some more rice.' She used to get instructions from Mama regarding the quantity and we managed. Mama was a great person that way; she had a lot of tact and was sincere, so no one took her amiss. She herself kept an open house and guests were well looked after.

While in Colombo we also stayed with Shankara Iyer. He was the sole agent for Sunlight soaps (made by Lever Brothers). The Iyers, a large family of four sons and four daughters, were rich and lived in a big bungalow. Their family genes seemed to have a curious streak. Out of a large family of eight children, two sons and two daughters were fair and handsome, another son and daughter were good-looking with a light complexion, while a son and a daughter were deformed, short and stunted. You could never say they belonged to the same family.

The story of how Shankara Iyer made his fortune is worth telling. Years ago a Chettiar, who was the sole agent then, employed Shankara Iyer in Lever Brothers as a clerk. Lever Brothers was a British firm. Shankara Iyer handled all the correspondence dealing with the firm, taking delivery of goods, accounts of sales, and other office matters. The poor Chettiar left everything in his hands, trusting him completely. There arose some occasion when the Chettiar quarrelled with Shankara Iyer and the latter resigned. Thereafter, when the Chettiar wrote on business matters to the British firm, they refused to recognize him as the authority with whom they were dealing. They wrote back saying that they only recognized Mr Shankara Iyer. So the Chettiar had to call Iyer back on his own terms and make him a partner. In course of time, Shankara Iyer took over the business completely and was made the sole agent for Sunlight.

Shankara Iyer's fourth daughter Muthu, who was about my age, was my friend. She had a physical deformity, but was intelligent and good in her studies. I met her, years later, when she came to Delhi. Daddy was also instrumental in bringing together the eldest daughter and her husband, who were estranged. The matter was that the Shankara Iyers were so stinking rich that they did not respect the son-in-law who came from a good family, but was not as rich. Daddy talked to the son-in-law and to the daughter and somehow settled their differences.

There were many other families whom we knew, but we did not stay with them.

As I have said earlier, many prominent personalities used to visit Kandy. Sri Krishnamurthy (editor of the popular magazine *Ananda Vikatan*), or Kalki as he is known, came with Mali, the well-known cartoonist of that magazine. Kalki later founded his own weekly magazine, *Kalki*. Daddy took them to some tea estates and told them about the problems, all the while requesting them not to mention his name as the source of information. Kalki asked a lot of probing questions to which Daddy would say, 'No, I won't tell you', and then go on to tell him much more than was asked. In the next few issues of *Ananda Vikatan*, Kalki published the first of a series of articles on his visit to Ceylon to the tea estates. It had a cartoon by Mali of Daddy holding up his forefinger and saying, 'I won't tell you.'

A group of schoolgirls and boys came with their teachers from a high school in Trichy. We all went in Daddy's car and another hired taxi to Hatton. On the way we halted for tiffin. The men managed to make *uppuma* and tea. I found the *uppuma* delicious, though others complained it was lumpy and salty. Among them was a girl Kamala whom I met years later in Delhi. She was a Hebbar Iyengar and was widowed soon after her marriage. She continued her studies in Trichy and came to Kandy with that group. She got married again to one

Mr Parthasarathy. I met her at Lodi Estate, when we were looking for a house after my third daughter, Jayashree, was born. She knew Mr M.S. Ramayyar (Deputy Accountant General) and put us in touch with him. We stayed with Mr Ramayyar for seven years in No. 77 Lodi Estate.

Krishna was already married to Pamanji, N. Ananthakrishnan, our Aunt Chellamma's son, and there was talk of Goma's marriage. Goma was promised to Ramaswamy, the son of Mama's elder brother R. Padmanabha Iyer. The elders had settled it among themselves. Ramaswamy Ammanji had it firmly fixed in his mind that he was going to marry Goma. Destiny came in his way. My parents came to know of another eligible boy, rich and handsome, who was the son of S. Mahadeva Iyer and a distant relative of ours. Soon after his appointment as the Dewan of Travancore, Mahadeva Iyer suddenly died, leaving behind his wife and two young sons. He was a wealthy man in those days, with properties right up to Cape Comorin. Apparently, he had donated jewels for Kanyakumari Devi, covering her from head to feet. He owned several bungalows and paddy lands. His family lived in a huge house in Sreevaraham, near the Fort area in Trivandrum. The house was divided later into two and given to each of the sons. Mahadeva Iyer's wife Gomathy was a very wise woman. She brought her sons up well and looked after the vast properties carefully, preserving them for the boys. It was said the lady was so courageous and resourceful that when her husband died all of a sudden, she had the presence of mind to go around the house locking up all the silver and the jewels and hide the keys before seeking outside help. She was well aware that in a society where the widow had to stay confined to one room surrounded by mourners, relatives as well as outsiders would have a field day stealing valuables from the house.

The elder son, M. Subramony, was a classmate of my brother and my cousin Ramaswamy. The younger son M. Padmanabhan also graduated. Both of them were handsome.

With all the wealth at their disposal, they had no need to work. My parents felt that Mony—short for Subramony—was a better catch for Goma than Ammanji (meaning cousin in Tamil), as cousin Ramaswamy was called by everyone. To the utter dismay of my mother's brother and sister-in-law and to the disappointment no doubt of Ramaswamy Ammanji, Goma's marriage was settled with Sreevaraham Mony. Another breach of faith committed by my parents was in settling Anantha's marriage with Saroja, granddaughter of my eldest Aunt Chellamma, and niece of my eldest brother-in-law Pamanji. There was an understanding that Goma would marry Ammanji and Anantha would marry Sarojem. My eldest uncle, Patha *mama* (R. Padmanabha Iyer), had a large family of four sons and five daughters. Sarojem was the fifth child.

Aunt Chellamma's daughter Gowri had one son Ramayya and a daughter Saroja. The daughter was also studying in Trivandrum and my brother and she must have known each other there. Then, when Anantha visited his aunt at Salem, he must have seen more of her there and come to like her. So Anantha told our parents that he would marry only Saroja. My mother was disappointed, as she thought she could patch up the misunderstanding caused by Goma's marriage to Mony, and cement the bond between the families by Anantha marrying Sarojem. But they had to give in to Anantha's wish, and his marriage to Saroja was celebrated in Alleppey.

At the time of Anantha's marriage, my youngest sister Sarasa was an infant of one year and four months. She used to go about with a nipple fitted to a feeding cup in her mouth, a plump sweet kid. We had a cook called Raman, whom we had brought with us to Alleppey for the wedding. Raman was the main player in an event that ever since is referred to, in our family, as the Raman Method. Sarasa was crying in the night and Mama had asked Raman to boil some water and bring it, as she thought the child might be crying because of thirst. When even after ten minutes no water came, Mama sharply asked Raman, 'Why do you take such a long time? Bring the hot water soon.' Raman came ceremoniously, cooling the water by pouring it out from the tumbler to the *davara* (a small flat vessel) and from the *davara* to the tumbler several times. Mama said, 'Give me the water, I will cool it.' But when she touched the water, it was absolutely cold. It was not hot water that Raman was cooling but cold water. The lazy fellow hadn't even lit the fire. Under cross-examination, he confessed to the truth. But, he was not a bad sort and was with us for some time.

I have to go back to Kandy, to the time when Goma was not married. Anantha was studying in Trivandrum; Krishna was married and was in Salem. Mama and Daddy used to make occasional trips to India. I don't know for what purpose, perhaps to scout for eligible boys for Goma or perhaps on some property matters. I was too young to know. Goma and I were left with Daddy's friend Mr T.S. Pillai.

Mr T.S. Pillai was a rich Jaffna Tamil. He was the first man to introduce town bus services in Kandy. He also had vast estates and other businesses. His wife was a sweet person, fair to the point of being nearly white, and it was said that she was an Anglo–Jaffna Tamil. They had three daughters and one young son of my age or perhaps a little younger. They had lost two sons very early. I remember the funeral processions passing through our street. Vignaraja was the only boy who survived, and he was the darling of the family.

The Pillais' house was on high ground. There were a number of steps leading to the house, which was surrounded by a large beautifully maintained garden. Behind the house there was hilly land covered with fruit trees. There were many nutmeg trees. Vignaraja and I used to pluck the nutmegs and eat them raw with salt. They had a tangy taste. The eldest daughter Daisy was also fair like her mother and was well built. She was good looking, but had a squint in her eyes. The next was Padma, who was a dark and serious girl; Leela was the youngest, a little older than Goma. She was the best looking of the three and was closest to Goma. We all went to the same school. The chauffeur-driven car used to drop us and bring us back. We enjoyed our stay with the Pillais. They were non-vegetarians, but vegetarian food was served for us. I have written before about the delicious Ceylonese food. We loved the food in the Pillais' house. Mr Pillai had a squeaky voice and would sometimes stand behind my chair and see that I ate properly. 'What is this Sethu pecking at her food like a bird?' he would say.

An old woman, whom they called *Aachi* (grandmother), would sometimes visit them. All of us would make fun of her, behind her back of course. I remember a jingle we had composed about her:

Aachi amma kone konde
Kakkusile periya chandai.
(Granny with the crooked hairdo
Fighting battles in the loo.)

Very silly and cruel of course, but that was the age to be silly. Another jingle was on the ayah, in English:

Ayah darling dimple dot
Cooking *kelangu* (yams) in the pot.

Goma and the others used to talk late into the night and laugh and giggle over what I could never understand, as I was kept out of all their secrets. Once their laughter became so uncontrollable that Mr Pillai had to come from his room and admonish them. They then stuffed the corners of their pillows into their mouths to stifle the noise.

We stayed with the Pillais two or perhaps three times. Mr Pillai used to call tantrics and holy men to the house, feed them, and give them money. Once a middle-aged Sinhalese man came. He had powers to see the future through a glass bottle, somewhat like crystal gazing. A table was placed in the centre of the room and a tall bottle of water set on it. Flowers and lighted agarbattis (incense sticks) were kept around the bottle. He first asked me to come and sit in a chair opposite the bottle and gaze for some time at it. He then said, 'If you see anything don't laugh at it or ridicule it, just tell us what you see.' Mr Pillai translated this to me in English. After gazing for five minutes, I saw the figure of a monkey. Impulsively, forgetting the warning, I blurted out, 'I see a monkey.' At once it disappeared and I could not see anything after that. No one else except Leela could see anything. She was able to see Lakshmi, Saraswati, and Hanuman. The man told her to ask them questions and get their replies. The proceedings were all in Sinhalese, and I did not understand a thing.

After some months, we heard rumours that Mr Pillai had lost all his money and property. He was arrested and taken to jail. One of my most painful memories is that of standing in our verandah in Arifa House and watching Mr Pillai, being taken through the street handcuffed. I think he underwent a term of imprisonment, though I am not sure about that.

I recall overhearing Daddy and Mama talking and gleaning scraps of information. It seems Mr Pillai stood surety for a large sum of money to an Indian, one Patel, who ran away to India without paying the debts and poor Mr Pillai had to incur losses and suffering. Their fortunes declined and they had to sell the big bungalow and take up residence in a small house. While we were in their house one Mr Somasundaram, an advocate, a balding middle-aged man, would visit. Daisy would be excited and would dress herself up. Goma, Leela, and Padma would tease her about him. They would use Latin words (Latin was their subject in school) so that I could be kept out of their conversation. I used to hover around trying to figure out what they were talking about, but I was always shooed away. Daisy married him and moved to a separate house. Mr Pillai had sold his house, so Daisy was married from our house. Daddy undertook a major part of the expense.

Padma married an Indian Air Force officer, and her marriage was also celebrated in Arifa House. I remember the date on which she married, 1 September 1939—the day England declared war on Germany.

Among Daddy's friends there were two others who were close to us. One was Mr Kalyanaraman of Hatton. His wife, a pretty young girl, came to Ceylon to join him and before going to Hatton she came to our house in Kandy. We hadn't yet moved to Arifa House. Mr Kalyanaraman was teaching in a school in Hatton. He was also a scout master. He took me to my first movie, a silent motion picture.

Then there was Dr Viswanathan in Balangoda tea estate. He hailed from Palghat in Kerala. Goma and I went to stay with him and his wife, when Daddy and Mama went to India on one of their visits. Daddy took us by car and left us at the outskirts of the estate. Dr Viswanathan had come with two coolies. He took charge of us, and Daddy went back. His house was two miles inside the estate, and we had to walk, with the coolies carrying our boxes. The whole place was full of leeches. I must have walked just a few hundred paces when one bit me. Blood flowed and the worm had to be pulled out. Dr Viswanathan then carried me on his shoulder till we reached his house. They had a nice house and Mrs Viswanathan was very kind. They had no children and the doctor treated his wife like a child, petting her and calling her darling. They used to play chess and if she was defeated, she would throw a tantrum and he would pacify her and say, 'Let's play another game. I think you were not concentrating.' She would win the next game, of course.

They had a cook, and breakfast every morning was rice *kanji* (gruel) with *aviyal* (a delicacy made with mixed vegetables cooked in a coconut base) or *paruppu* (lentil) *kootu* or some other vegetable preparation. Dr Viswanathan and his wife were fond of Goma and me, and I was happy staying with them.

In Kandy we had a family doctor, Dr Sreenivasan. His wife
Kantimathy was a beautiful woman. They were a loving
couple, but perhaps they were ill starred as they lost three
boys. Only one daughter, Rukmani, survived. One son
Jayaraman was studying in Benares Engineering College, when
he died suddenly. The other two died young. They were
shattered and miserable, so Daddy brought them home to stay
with us. Mrs Sreenivasan would weep all the time and was
inconsolable. The doctor used to sit near her, comb her long
hair lovingly, and comfort her. It was so sad to see them suffer.
He was a competent doctor, but had an awful temper and if
his instructions were not carried out he would shout at the
patient. Still, his clinic was always crowded. They lived in a
flat above the clinic. Rukmani was my age and she would come
many times with their Sinhalese servant girl, Soma, to play
with me. There is a picture somewhere in our album of
Rukmani, Soma and myself with our dog Muglis. Muglis was
a fat puppy and a glutton. In our family, anything fat came
to be called Muglis; even a bulky letter brought by the
postman was referred to as a 'Muglis.'

When we were in Ghafoor House, Krishna had a pet
pussycat. The only person who cared for the cat was Krishna,
and the cat fully reciprocated her love. No one else liked even
the sight of the pussy. She would follow Krishna to school up
to the gates, then return home. She was a wicked creature,
stealing milk if she could get to it. Mama tried to drive her
away and asked the peon to take her away to some far-off place
and leave her, but the next day, she would be back at home. It
was incredible the way pussy found her way home. Krishna
would try to protect her. She raised a storm when she heard
of Mama's attempts to drive it out. But Mama was equally
determined to get rid of the creature somehow. Our washerman
Michael used to come on Sundays. One Sunday Mama put
pussy in a gunny bag and asked Michael to take her away with
him and that was the last we heard of pussy. Krishna made a

scene and cried, but Mama said 'no pets in the house' and that was that.

Strangely of all the children only Krishna had a love for animals. Her husband Pamanji also loved animals. In their home in Salem, Pamanji Anna had a monkey for a pet. Our paternal grandmother Kalyani Patti (*patti* in Tamil means grandmother) was also in Salem. She had become blind since she developed cataract in both her eyes, but she stoutly refused to have them removed by operation. In those days cataract surgery was a painful process, entailing many days of absolute bed rest.

One day Kalyani Patti—who was also Pamanji's maternal grandmother—was sitting and distributing bananas to everyone. She gave one to Pamanji. He said he did not want it. She insisted, and cajoling him to eat the fruit, peeled the skin and held out her hand for him to take the fruit. Pamanji had left by then, but the monkey was sitting there and obediently took the fruit from her hand. Patti was very happy and said, 'There, I knew you would like it, have some more', and peeled another banana. The monkey gratefully accepted it. The third one was in the process of being handed over when someone happened to come to the room and exclaimed, 'Patti, whom are you feeding the bananas to?' Patti chuckled, 'Pamanji said he won't have it, so I am peeling the fruit and giving it to him.' There was a loud burst of laughter that drew the household out. Patti was indignant when told that it was the monkey she had been feeding all this while. She abused the monkey left, right, and centre. But by then, he had taken his leave.

Another incident told by Daddy related to the Sinhalese. The Sinhalese people were said to be impulsive and hotheaded. They were heavy drinkers and drunken brawls on the street were a common sight.

There was a Sinhalese overseer in a tea estate. The overseer had worked in the estate for more than fifteen years and was trusted and liked by the superintendent, an Englishman. It occurred to the Englishman that this man should be rewarded. So he called him and announced an increment which would effectively double his income and commended him for his excellent work. The immediate reaction of this Sinhalese overseer was to whip out a knife and stab the superintendent, shouting in Sinhalese, 'So you have been denying me an increment all these years? Too late now for you to reward me.' The superintendent died, and the Sinhalese faced the consequences of his dastardly act.

Two other incidents come to my mind. My second class teacher in school was Miss Perera. She was a short woman with protruding teeth. She was a good teacher, and we all liked her class. She lived in our street a few yards further down and on the opposite side. Our peon Banda used to call her by the nickname Bathalakodi, meaning 'betel leaf creeper' because she was slim.

One year on Christmas Eve, Banda came running with the shocking news of a shooting in Miss Perera's house. It seems she was the eldest of eleven children. On Christmas Eve, the family sat down to dinner—eleven children and the father and mother making it thirteen. Half way through the meal Mr Perera who was sozzled with drink, took out his revolver and shot Mrs Perera, then shot himself. There was a big crowd outside the house till the police came and took charge. Next morning, it was a front-page story in all the newspapers. Drinking was the bane of the Sinhalese. After a month, Miss Perera came back to her teaching.

The second incident had occurred sometime earlier. There was a woman selling *kiri kos* (jackfruit), carrying the fruit in a basket on her head, with a big carving knife to cut the fruit. We used to buy fruit from her. She was a tall, gaunt woman; she tied her sarong tightly round her waist with the bottom end tucked into her waist to facilitate movement. She did not walk, but rather took large strides shouting '*kiri kos, kiri kos.*' Her hair was tied in a small tight knot at the back of her head. She looked masculine and was stronger than many men.

We used to call her Kiri Kos. She lived in a one-room quarter, just a little further down our house. This small room was wedged in between two big bungalows. Perhaps the room was originally intended as a kennel: it was such a small room. We could see her in the evening, cooking and chatting with her husband, an equally unsavoury-looking character. One day, it was dusk when we heard shouts. A big crowd had gathered in front of her hovel. We came to know that both husband and wife were drunk and quarrelling, and in a fit of anger Kiri Kos took out her big cutting knife and cut off her husband's head—beheaded him. People told us about the gory sight of his bleeding head. They said when the police came to take Kiri Kos away in handcuffs she went boldly, shouting curses. For many days, I was afraid even to look in the direction of her room.

The Sinhalese were not enterprising as a people. Without the labour of the migrant groups, especially the industries built up by Indian and Jaffna Tamils, Sri Lanka would not have developed into a prosperous island with an export trade in tea, rubber, *copra*, and mica.

Then there were the Burghers, descendants of the Dutch and the Portuguese who had come to Ceylon in the sixteenth or seventeenth century and settled there. They married the local Sinhalese and their children came to be called Burghers. Besides these Burghers and the Tamils (inclusive of both the Jaffna Tamils and the Tamils from India) were the Moors, the Muslims who had come from the Middle East and Malaya to settle in Sri Lanka.

The Sinhalese cultural identity was largely derived from their religion. Buddhism was their official faith and they celebrated *Perehera*, *Vesak* (*Buddha Purnima*), and Christmas. *Vesak* is celebrated not only in Ceylon, but in other Buddhist countries as well. It falls on the full moon day in May. It is a day which commemorates Lord Buddha's birth, enlightenment, and nirvana. On such days, Kandy's streets and houses were decorated with festoons and colourful lanterns. Tableaux depicting various scenes from the life of Lord Buddha were set up outside the houses. Of course, prayers, visits to Buddhist viharas, temples, feasting, and distribution of sweets were all part of the festivities.

The upper-class Sinhalese were very westernised in their way of life, though women wore the sari in the Sinhalese fashion, like a dhoti having a little gather at the left end and a two-inch frill hanging out with a short upper cloth. The young girls wore it the same way with a blouse, but without an upper cloth.

The European colonial influence had a curious effect on the lifestyles of the Sinhalese, seen particularly in their names. Almost all of them had Christian names, only their surnames were Sinhalese. For instance, a former Prime Minister, the late S.W.R.D. Bandaranaike was named Solomon West Ridgeway Dias Bandarnaike. Another former Prime Minister was Sir John Kotelewala. A former High Commissioner to India was Sir Edwin Viyayaratne. These are only to name a few. If the Sinhalese men were hard drinkers, the Burghers were worse. A popular tongue-twister about the Burghers ran like this:

Burgher buggers buying buying
Brandy bottles became beggars

Dutch names like van Lebrugan and van Dermot as also Portuguese names like De Soysa, De Silva, De Mello and De Janey were common among the Sinhalese. In contrast to the Sinhalese and Burghers, the Jaffna Tamils were mild mannered, but were accused of being deep and cunning.

The Sinhalese had a good Ayurvedic system of medicine. Herbs and plants with curative qualities abounded in Kandy. When my younger sister Padha was one or one and a half years old, she fell seriously ill with double pneumonia. She had high fever and a congested lung condition for more than a month. Apart from the family doctor who was treating her, Daddy brought in a specialist, Dr Spittiel, head of the Kandy Government Hospital, to see her. He was not satisfied with her condition at all and held not much hope of a recovery. Penicillin and other antibiotics had not yet been discovered. The only treatment for pneumonia was application of anti-phlagistin, which came in a three-inch round aluminium tin. I still have one these—a mustard-based ointment applied hot on lint and plastered on the chest and the back with a dry fomentation of heated bran or bricks wrapped in towels.

The poor child's back and sides were blistered with the application. The household was tense after Dr Spittiel's visit. Mama was so agitated, she prayed all the time. Our Sinhalese peon Banda came hesitantly to Mama and begged her to give him permission to bring a *Vaid* to see the child. He pleaded that since the great English doctor had said it was a hopeless case 'why not try an Ayurvedic cure?' He vouchsafed for Nandisenan, the *Vaid* who had treated his children and whom he personally knew. His arguments convinced Mama, but she did not tell Daddy as he was a staunch believer in allopathy and would not have given permission. Banda brought Dr Nandisenan, a Sinhalese with a tuft (all orthodox Sinhalese tied their long hair in a knot) and a curved comb on top of it; he wore a sarong. I distinctly remember his face. He felt Padha's pulse, examined her thoroughly and said that within 48 hours the fever would come down if the powder he gave was administered faithfully. Banda went with him and brought back the eight doses of the powder with instructions to administer each dose in a spoonful of orange juice. The orange was of a particular variety called *dhodang* in Sinhalese and it was dark green and sour. It was nothing short of a miracle when the fever came down to 99 degrees within 48 hours. The *Vaid* came again and prescribed other powders, and Padha turned the corner and recovered gradually. Mama had implicit faith in

Nandisenan, and even for my first baby I gave his coriander seed pellets for cold and fever.

Padha was very fair like Daddy and a sweet child. But the serious illness she went through made everyone indulgent towards her. All her whims were fulfilled. She became disobedient and gave Mama a lot of trouble. She became so unmanageable that when our Aunt Ammulu came over on one of her visits, she took Padha with her and put her in a boarding school in Bangalore run by Lady Raman, wife of Sir C.V.Raman. She was there for a few months. When the poor child became homesick she was brought back. But the absence from home tamed her only a bit. She continued to be a self-willed child.

In 1933 or 1934 there was an epidemic of a virulent type of malaria which raged through some parts of the island. Kandy was most badly affected. People just dropped down on the streets while walking or cycling and had to be taken in an ambulance to hospitals. The government hospitals were over-crowded. There was not a home in Kandy which was not hit by the epidemic. There were no vendors on the road. Milk was in short supply as the milkmen were down with fever. Daddy, Mama, Goma and my two younger sisters were all down with the dreaded malarial disease. I was the only one who did not fall sick; perhaps I had a built-in resistance to mosquitoes. Even the servants were too ill to attend to their duties. I had to make rice gruel or tea or whatever the patients wanted. I was then not yet ten. Quinine in its rawest form was prescribed, both as a preventive and as a cure. It was a small yellow tablet and terribly bitter. It was also said that an overdose of quinine could cause deafness because of its unrefined form. Nowadays it comes in a more palatable form. The bitterness would linger in the mouth and throat for days. Even food tasted bitter. Mama and Goma were the worst affected. Their temperature would go shooting up to 105 degrees or 106 degrees Celsius. We would pile all the available blankets and mattresses over them. But the fever came only on alternate days, a peculiar symptom of this particular form of malaria. The next day there would be no fever, but the patient would be quite weak. The epidemic raged for two to three weeks and then subsided.

After conditions became normal my eldest sister Krishna and brother-in-law Pamanji came to Kandy. When they returned to Salem, I went back with them for a change during my December holidays. In Ceylon we did not know much about the freedom struggle and the Indian National Congress. But when I was in Salem, I came to know something of what was going on. I learnt some of the patriotic songs that were sung defying the British ban on such songs.

Many of the songs were in Hindi, but were sung by people in the south as well—there were no anti-Hindi feelings then. My aunt Chellamma's husband, Dr Narayana Iyer, whom we never saw as he died at the age of 38, was a staunch Congressman. He was a friend and the family doctor of C. Rajagopalachari, who eventually became Governor General and then Chief Minister of Tamil Nadu. We, like many other families, wore only home-spun cloth. Many south Indian women joined the Congress and were involved in the freedom struggle. Many of them went to prison. I remember a family friend, Kamakshi Natesan, from a conservative Brahmin family who was arrested and jailed for her patriotic activities.

Anantha was the eldest born and being the only son he should have been pampered and petted. But strangely, the girls were more indulged in. After his schooling in Kandy, Anantha was sent to Trivandrum for his Inter and B.A. from Madras University, which had a name from Trivandrum to Ganjam. He was full of fun and mischief.

We were in Ghafoor House when he had come home for his holidays. His Intermediate results were expected any day. In those days, since there were not many students, the names of those who passed were published in the local papers. *The Hindu* published the Madras University results. That memorable day Anantha was upstairs, amusing us by tying an empty wooden bobbin to a long string and letting it drop on passers-by. All those who were passing that area were given a gentle knock on the head with the wooden reel, dexterously manipulated from above by Mr S.A. Krishnan like a puppeteer handling the strings. The recipients of this favour were the servant maid, Aunt Ammulu, and my mother. They would look up to see where the knock came from, but wouldn't sight anyone.

In the midst of these operations, Daddy came home and from downstairs he shouted 'Ananthakrishna!' When Daddy was angry with Anantha, he called him by his full name. All was silence; Mama came hurriedly to see what the commotion was about. Daddy was shouting, 'Where is that good-for-nothing fellow?' Anantha had to go down and stand like a sheep waiting for the slaughter. Daddy had a copy of *The Hindu* with him and was pointing to the Inter results, where one name was not on the list. Anantha had failed that year. For some days after this, all joyful activities were at a standstill. My brother crept about with a deeply injured air, as if to say that the world was treating him badly. He had to go back and repeat his second year. He did pass his Inter and B.A. though in the 'royal class' as the Third Class was referred to in those days.

My husband, who is also my cousin, used to narrate to me my brother's exploits in college where they studied together. My brother had a brilliant intellect and a phenomenal memory. But, all his talents were directed towards inventing games to make his teachers' lives miserable. He adopted the mass participation technique, so that no one individual could be singled out for punishment. The teachers suspected that Mr S.A.K. was the root cause of all the rowdyism, but had no proof. One of the games played in class whenever anyone was punished was to start a refrain, '*Paavam*', meaning 'poor thing.' The whole class would quickly echo the refrain and the strains would reach the next classroom, where it would be taken up. Wave after wave of the refrain would go on till the volume became so low that it could not be taken up. The nuisance was in sympathetic reaction to a class fellow being sent out of class. All the teachers from all the classrooms would come out and there would be a conference, but a crowd of a hundred or more students cannot be taken to task, unless they are dismissed for the day, which would be a boon instead of a punishment!

My brother stayed in the hostel. According to him rules were meant to be broken. The rule that set the lights-off time at 10.00 p.m. was not applicable to my brother and his friends. A good cinema being shown at the theatre was sufficient excuse for them to slip out through the window, leaving their beds made with artistic humps resembling a sleeping body covered with blankets and pillows. The warden would make his round at about 10.30 p.m. and, finding everything normal, would quietly go away.

My brother's phenomenal memory once stood him in good stead. The teacher was reading out a passage from the English text, when he happened to look up from his book and find one gentleman's attention wandering. The teacher asked Mr S.A.K., the culprit, to read out the passage he had just read. Mr S.A.K picked up a book from his desk, stood up, and read out the passage word for word. The teacher came up to him and looked at the book he was reading from: it was a mathematics textbook. My brother did not have his English textbook with him. The teacher was astounded and went back to his table without saying a word. It was this quality in him—his brilliance—that made the teachers overlook his other crimes. In contrast to him, his cousin Ramaswamy was a well-behaved, studious young man. The cousins, though poles apart in nature, were fond of each other, as they had grown up together.

During festival days, Anantha would go with his cousins to their house. The feasting was welcome to him, but not the rituals. He avoided going to his uncle's house on such occasions, but once found himself at their house on *Avani Avittam* day, which also happened to be his birthday. On this day Brahmins change their holy thread and atone for all the sins committed unknowingly. The priest would come to the house and the *brahmacharis* as well as married Brahmins had to change their holy thread and perform a *homam* (offering of oblations to the sacred fire). This festival falls on the full moon day in the month of August. In the North they celebrate it as *Raksha Bandhan*, a day when sisters tie threads on their brother's wrist and brothers vow to protect them. The priest asked Anantha his *Gotra*, which defines the lineage of the person concerned from a particular sage. Anantha whispered, 'It doesn't matter, go ahead.' But the conscientious priest would not budge till Anantha had announced his *Gotra*. By that time all the elders came to know of the dilemma and more senior people were consulted and family trees traced to find out poor Anantha's *Gotra*. At last it was declared to be *Haritha Gotra* and the ceremonies were completed. That was the first and last time Mr S.A.K. went to his uncle's house on *Avani Avittam* day.

My school days were threatening to come to a close. There was talk of going to Trivandrum to fix up my marriage with my cousin Ramaswamy. I was now next in line to be married and my parents were getting anxious, as I was already ten years old. In those days, girls had to be married off before they attained puberty and I was on the threshold of puberty! My uncle's son Ramaswamy was the only eligible boy in the family, but my parents knew they would have to face a hostile atmosphere in my uncle's house because of their breach of faith in the case of the earlier alliances that should have taken place with my uncle's family. Daddy, Mama, and I went to Trivandrum in April 1935.

I had two maternal uncles staying in Trivandrum. My younger uncle, R. Krishnaswamy Iyer, lived in East Fort Street inside the Fort. He had no children. It seems his wife,

Aunt Bhagavathy, did conceive, but the delivery was complicated. In those days the Caesarean method was unknown. And the lady doctor, perhaps not competent enough to handle such a case, messed up everything and the baby had to be taken out in pieces to save the mother. Aunt Bhagavathy could never conceive after that.

My elder uncle, R. Padmanabha Iyer, lived in a place called Taikad. He had a large family of four sons and five daughters. My Aunt Kalyani had lost two boys aged one and a half and two years, and had one or two stillborns and abortions.

My eldest cousin was Krishnambal; the second was Devaki, called Thevoo by all; and then Ramaswamy, called Ammanji; and another son Subrahmaniam, also called Mani. After Mani followed two daughters, Sarojem and Ambujam, and two sons Lakshman and Sundaram. The last child, Sarada, was born after my marriage. Since I was being considered for Ramaswamy, we were staying in Uncle Krishna's house in Fort. On a Friday, an auspicious day for such expeditions, I went with my parents to be 'seen' by my uncle, aunt and the person concerned, in other words, to be approved of as a bride.

By coincidence, my mother's cousin Pichu had also brought her granddaughter Rama for the same purpose. Rama was older than I was and of very fair complexion. She was better suited in age for my cousin. But God had created an ally in my aunt's father whom everyone called Kunjaman *appa*. He was blind with a cataract, which he wouldn't allow to be removed, and remained blind till the end. He made me sit on his lap and felt my face. The choice was now between my rival and me, the fair girl and the dark girl. After the visit we returned to Fort. I wish I had asked my husband what went on in their house about the decision. Somehow I never asked him.

Even after three or four days, the decision was not conveyed to my parents. Meanwhile I was having a good time, visiting temples, going to my sister Goma's house in Sreevaraham, and singing with Aunt Bhagavathy. She was a sweet person and loved music. I was not in the least bothered about my marriage. Girls of my age those days were precocious and knew all about getting married, but I was an innocent nitwit. Even when my aunt hinted that perhaps the people at Taikad were thinking of the elder son being fixed for Rama and the younger son for me, I could not care less about whom I married as long as there was a good time to be had. The idea must have been dropped immediately, as there was no further talk and anyway Mani was too young to get married. Well, Mama and Daddy must have been on pins and needles, since they were going daily to Taikad. My mother was the youngest of my grandfather's children through his first wife Krishnambal and was a favourite with my uncle. But, there was a hostile atmosphere among the younger people as the two alliances settled earlier with our family were broken. This rankled a lot. I was told it was Kunjaman *appa* who settled the issue by declaring that Anandam's daughter Sethu should be fixed for Ramaswamy. My parents were there that evening, and my mother, who was a diplomat par excellence, asked Ammanji if he would buy his own wedding suit or should they buy it. It seems he muttered, 'I shall buy it.' Within five minutes my mother and father took their leave and went away jubilantly. Perhaps I had a priority over my rival Rama, as I was a *Murapenn* (alliances between first cousins—children of a brother and sister—had a priority over other alliances).

There was a Nair maidservant, Bhagirathi, in my uncle's house in Taikad who was with the family for a long time. I remember Bhagirathi as a short, slim woman who wore her long hair in a curious elongated knot jutting out four or five inches at the back. She would always be chattering, shaking her head vigorously in approval or disapproval, with her pyramidal knot shaking along with her head. I was fascinated by it. She had only one son, named Appu, but three husbands. In those days in Kerala, many of the Malayali working class women were polyandrous. I find that polyandry also prevails among the people of Kinnaur in Himachal Pradesh. A family of three or four sons would share a wife, keeping up the tradition of Draupadi, who was wife to all five of the Pandava brothers. There are temples to Draupadi in Himachal Pradesh, as well as in Kerala and Tamil Nadu.

Bhagirathi's salary was Rs 2.50 per month. It seems incredible that in 1934 a human being could not only subsist, but also support a family on a wage of two rupees per month. Sixty years ago living was cheap. One did not need money to spend on consumer goods. In Kerala, people walked without footwear. Before going to Ceylon, my father was earning the princely sum of nineteen rupees per month in the Government Secretariat.

Bhagirathi had been with the family for a long time and she was loyal to them. Her loyalty extended to her involvement in family affairs. She once overheard my parents discussing the alliance and remarking: 'Ammanji looks like a lamb, but he can be a veritable tiger when aroused,' and promptly conveyed the same to my aunt. Ammanji must have carried a lot of resentment over the broken alliances. After my marriage was settled, no 'terms' such as dowry were discussed. But my parents, not wishing to put my uncle to any expense gave Rs 3,000 towards the expenses, apart from gold jewellery, silver and brass vessels, and furniture. Silk saris and dhotis were given for the sambandhis, the family to be related by marriage. My wedding bed and wardrobe which were given latter were made of rosewood. Travancore was rich in timber. Rosewood, mahogany, and ebony furniture was cheap.

The wedding was fixed for 7 June 1935. A house was rented for a month near my uncle's house in Taikad. There were two buildings opposite each other and a big ground in the centre. One building was set apart for the wedding ceremonies, and we stayed in the smaller building. My mother and father were busy with the arrangements; some relatives had come to help with the cooking. My second sister-in-law-to-be, Thevoo Akka, used to come to see us on her way home after her bath in the temple tank. She would be wrapped in a wet sari with a lot of washed clothes on her shoulder. She was a tall and beautiful lady, with an aquiline nose and long hair. Her husband Ayya Athimber was a landlord in a village called Krishnapuram, a night's journey from Trivandrum. Her husband and mother-in-law were her only family, he being a posthumous child. After he died, for a year they spared the poor lady the cruel custom of shaving the head and wearing white. At the age of 19 she was disfigured with the stamp of widowhood. Her son grew up to be an idealist. He was a Congressman and took part in the freedom struggle as a Gandhian. In those days there were some who did not believe in the Mahatma's theory of non-violence and indulged in terrorism. Some of the Brahmins in Krishnapuram village were involved in murder and acts of violence. Sister Thevoo had a son Shankaran, the same age as my cousin Sundaram, and a daughter Kalyani. Her second daughter Padama was born after my marriage.

I remember my cousin Ramaswamy cycling down to our house. I can see him leaning on his bike and talking to Mama. He had come to offer his services. Mama was pleased with this gesture, but told him that since the wedding was only a week away, he should not be seen visiting us. He was the bridegroom elect now and not a nephew. I watched all this from a window and thought how handsome he was!

Weddings in those days were a five-day affair. The first day was the *Janavasam*, in which the bride's party invited the groom and his party. This was done with the *Mangalavadya*, auspicious music, being played on the piped instrument, *nadhaswaram*, by the *nadhaswaram vidwan* and his troupe. The procession went all the way from my house to the bridegroom's house. The ladies carried huge plates of fruits, betel leaves, betelnuts, candy, and dry fruits. They also carried a pair of huge cone-shaped sweets. One was made of cashewnuts and sugar, and the other was of *laddoos,* both cast in conical moulds and wrapped with silver paper and decorated with flowers. For every occasion during the marriage, a new pair of cones with different stuffing were kept in the centre of the decorated marriage podium. The formal betrothal ceremony took place that night.

The second day was the wedding day. In the morning after the *mangala snanam* or holy bath, the bride and the groom, had to go through the rituals of *nama karanam* and *vrata.* In the morning, the entertaining ritual of *Kasi Yatra* was performed. This is a little drama the groom is supposed to enact, saying that if this girl was not given to him in marriage he would go away to the Holy Land of Benaras, or Kasi, to become an ascetic. The groom would discard his fine clothes, wear a simple dhoti, and pick up a wooden staff, umbrella, and a holy book in his hand. He would then wear wooden sandals and turn his steps towards the Holy Land for *tapas.* The bride's father would go after the groom and beg him to turn back, as he was willing to give him his daughter's hand in marriage. He would hold the groom's hands and bring him back. My cousin went through all this, and I watched him coyly.

The bride would then come and garland the bridegroom and people would have some fun on this occasion, too. The maternal uncles of the bride and groom would carry their niece and nephew on their shoulders. Just as the bride would be about to put the garland round the groom's neck, they would whisk the groom back a few feet and let the bride's uncle chase him. Then it would be the turn of the bride's uncle to show his prowess. Krishna *mama* carried me on his shoulder and Suppu *mama* carried Ramaswamy. After some time, the officiating priest would put a stop to the fun by saying that the auspicious time was nearing. When all this was done at my wedding, I remember the groom losing his balance and holding onto me while getting down from his uncle's shoulder. This provoked a big guffaw from the delighted crowd and remarks like, 'Ammanji is already leaning on his wife for support,' were made. The bridal pair could be carried on the shoulders in those days, as they were very young. I was 10 years old and my cousin 21, a doll of a girl and a slip of a lad.

The first physical contact occurred when we were asked to hold our right hands together. This was *panigrahanam*, literally 'taking the hand.' After this came the *oonjal* (swing) ceremony. A plank was hung by hooks from the ceiling. The bride and bridegroom were made to sit on it as the ladies sang and gently rocked the swing. Then the bride's mother, the groom's mother, aunts and elder ladies from both sides went around the couple, carrying water for sprinkling on the ground, lighted oil lamps, and balls of red and yellow rice. One by one, the ladies took the plates of rice balls and went around the couple three times. Taking one red and one yellow rice ball, they waved their hands round the couple and flung the balls to the right. Another pair of yellow and red rice balls was waved around the couple and flung to the left; another was thrown behind the couple and another in front of them. It was said to ward off the evil eye and provide protection. All this time it was the head priest's job to see that the time schedule was kept. He hurried the women to finish all these minor ceremonies, so that he could get on to the important ceremony of *kanyadhanam,* i.e., giving away the bride, which has to be done within the auspicious time. After this, the *koorai,* the nine-yard wedding sari, and the *tirumangalyam* were placed on a plate and handed round to be blessed by the assembled elders. The *tirumangalyam* represents an ancient Tamil marriage custom. The groom ties a turmeric-dipped thread to which the sacred pendant, *taali,* is strung marking the completion of the ceremony. The groom's eldest sister had to help the bride in wearing the nine-yard sari in the traditional way for the *thali* ceremony. My eldest sister-in-law Krishnambal Akka tied the sari for me with my sister Goma assisting. I was so thin that I could hardly keep the sari in place. After being made to wear a thick rose garland, I was escorted back into the *pandal* and the groom was already dressed in a silk dhoti in the *panchakacham* style, the traditional Brahmin way of wearing the dhoti after marriage. Then the priests from both sides chanted mantras thrice with the *Gotram* and lineage of the girl and boy. First, the priest from the girl's side, then in reply the priest from the boy's side. This is one of the most beautiful parts of the Brahmin wedding ceremony. Following this, a bundle of straw was spread like a seat and my father sat on it, and I was made to sit on his lap. The priest chanted the *kanyadhana mantras*, and my mother poured the water to sanctify the gift. The groom was invoked as Maha Vishnu, since the *kanyadhanam* was always to Maha Vishnu even among *Smarthas* like us.

To the accompaniment of a crescendo of music from the *nadhaswaram* and the drum, played to a fast tempo and at a high pitch as if in a grand finale, the bridegroom tied the yellow thread with the gold *tirumangalyam* round my neck. Krishnambal Akka strengthened the knot her brother had tied round my neck with two more knots. The assembled crowd showered rose petals and flowers on us.

The last major part of the marriage ceremony was the *saptapadi*, literally 'seven steps' that the couple take round the fire, with a corner of the bridegroom's dhoti being tied to a corner of the bride's sari. The Sanskrit mantras chanted are essentially a set of instructions for the young couple poised on the threshold of married life. The wordings are both powerful and beautiful, and I give below a broad translation of the text of the *saptapadi*, in which the husband tells the wife,

> *May Lord Vishnu follow the first step to bless us with*
> *bounty for our sustenance;*
> > *And with our second step, too, may He follow us*
> *in order to bless us with strength and wealth;*

> *Accompanying you on your third step, may He bless*
> *us so we may perform all rituals and observances that*
> *are good and holy;*
> *Ever with you, may Lord Vishnu bless us, with your*
> *fourth step, with every joy and happiness, fulfilling our*
> *desires and bringing us contentment;*
> *May He follow this fifth step of yours so we may*
> *be blessed with the bountiful wealth of cows;*
> *Then let the blessings of the proper seasons too*
> *come from him with this, your sixth step;*
> *And with Lord Vishnu accompanying you on your*
> *seventh step, may He then bestow upon us the merits*
> *acquired from the performance of all that is holy and*
> *good by both our families.*

After the *saptapadi*, my husband, holding my hand, took me outside the *pandal* and showed me the star Arundhati. Of course, it was broad daylight and we could not possibly see any star, but it was convention, and I dutifully said that I could see Arundhati. The significance of this was that the couple should live like Arundhati and Rishi Vasishta. After this both of us performed *homam* every day for the next three days.

In South India, the marriage ceremony for Brahmins is different from that for the other castes. One thing common to all the communities in the south is the tying of the sacred thread, or *taali*, in Tamil, which is the *tirumangalyam* in Sanskrit. The Kasi *yatra*, seeing Arundhati, and the *saptapadi* are, however, Brahmanical customs mostly from the *Yajur Veda*, and the mantras are chanted in Sanskrit.

The crowds had dispersed for lunch or on other business. The priest, a few elders and the newlyweds were the only people in the *pandal*. In Trivandrum, the decoration of the *pandal* was an art form. The roof was made of white cloth with gold and silver stars glittering on it. Around the *pandal* were artistic balconies, like they have in palaces, painted so as to create an illusion of a corridor and rooms inside. I don't think they have this type of decorated *pandal* anywhere else in India. The pandals for the royal weddings, called *Palli Kattu*, were like this but decorated on a much grander scale.

In the afternoon of the wedding day, after lunch, there is a ceremony called *Nalangu*. Ceremonies like this have been invented just to provide friends and relatives with an occasion to tease the newlyweds and have fun. I was supposed to go and invite my husband to come play *Nalangu* with me. I wore a six-yard sari and with some of my relatives we went to the bridegroom's room. My husband was sitting on a table, dangling his legs, surrounded by his friends. When I came and stood there, his friends egged him on and asked him to insist on my singing or refuse to come. Little did they know that I was not some shy village girl to make a fuss about singing. I would have gladly teased them myself, if not for the restraints laid on me by my sisters, who knew that I was capable of anything. They had strictly told me to be shy and modest, and walk with my head down and not skip and run as I was wont to. Remembering that, I kept silent, stealing a glance at my cousin. It seemed to me that he did not want to bully me into singing, but his friends were too vociferous for him to ignore. So he said in English, 'If you sing a song, I'll come.' I was about to render a *kirtanam*, when his friends shouted, 'No, no. A song in English.'

Just before my marriage, a music teacher was engaged to teach me a few songs. He taught me a few classical songs as well as an English song. So I sang:

> 'Cotton land is in jubilation, cotton land is in Coronation.
>
> For every one is in cotton area for the crowning of the Cotton Queen.
>
> Don't forget that you are all invited to the crowning of the Cotton Queen.

> *Cotton suits, cotton coats, every kind of cotton
> clothes.*
> *For the crowning of the Cotton Queen.'*

From where the *bhagavatar* picked up this song God alone
knows. Since this was the only song in English I knew apart
from hymns, I sang this and at the end was given a round of
applause. 'His Majesty' came with me for the *Nalangu*.
Only recently did I come to know that the song had been
composed and sung by one of our famous musicians,
Ariyyakkudi Ramanuja Iyengar, on the Duke of Gloucester's
visit to India.

Nalangu is an interesting ceremony that originated
with child marriages, although mature adults go through the
same ceremony today with somewhat comic effects. A silk mat
was spread. The bridegroom and I sat at opposite ends facing
each other. A brass ball the size and shape of a coconut with
stones put in it to make a noise was rolled from the bride to
the groom and back. Then a pot of water with a ring in it was
kept at the centre, and we were asked to take the ring out.
There was a tussle, with our hands touching in the water
while fishing for the ring. I then had to smear sandal paste on
him and he did the same. Then we crushed roasted *papads* on
each other's head. A lot of fun and laughter and singing
completed the merriment. The lyrics of many of the *Nalangu*
songs were vulgar, abounding in double entendre. I do not
know whether this was meant to educate or titillate the bridal
couple. All this must have been fun when the bride and
the groom were children. I was ten, but it is somewhat
ridiculous that *Nalangu* should continue in this era of late
marriages!

In the evening there was the *patna pravesam*, literally 'going
around the city.' A car was decorated with flowers with the
hood down, and my husband and I were taken in a slow
procession to the Fort area. All the kids, as many as could be

managed, piled into the car with us, and friends and relatives walked along. The car crawled at a snail's pace. It stopped at every relative's house where the lady of the house came up to us and gave us milk with pieces of plantain fruit in it, three spoonfuls in the palm of our hands. *Aarti* would be performed and the car would move on to the next house. I don't think we spoke to each other at all during the drive. Getting to know each other was a long process. It took us a year before we spoke freely to each other.

The third day of the marriage was the same with *homam* in the morning and *Nalangu* in the afternoon. In the evening there was a *Hari Katha* by Sri E.V. Narayana Bhagavatar, who was related to us. The story told was *Sita Kalyanam*. The fourth day's schedule was the same in the morning and afternoon. In the evening, a young girl and her brother gave a music concert. It was good and on both occasions we were asked to give the artists presents.

The fifth and last day of the marriage festivities was *Sesha Homam*, the final *homam*. During lunch the *sambandhis,* or the bridegroom's party, were sprayed with coloured water and ribald songs were sung, describing the groom's mother as a lady with a red nose, short skimpy hair and a big wart . . . It was all taken in good sport with mock quarrels and embraces. In the evening, the farewell function was held, thanks were given, gifts exchanged, and dinner packed in huge baskets. Vegetables, fruits, pulses, sugar and everything needed for cooking was also packed. To the accompaniment of pipes, they were given a warm and hearty send-off. One interesting aspect of my marriage was that my mother would consult her *manni* (sister-in-law) about everything. My mother-in-law would come to our house, arrange everything, give all instructions, and go back to her house to assume the role of *sambandhi.* My mother's mother died when my mother was only three years old, so she was practically brought up by her eldest brother and sister-in-law.

And so Sethu got married to her cousin Ramaswamy and lived with him happily for 57 years. I was a child-bride at ten, a wife at thirteen, and a mother at fifteen.

I have written in detail about my five-day wedding ceremonies, because today weddings are a one-day function. Mine was the last child marriage in my family because the Sharada Act, which forbade such marriages, followed soon after. My younger sisters Padma and Sarasa were educated and working when they got married although they also had arranged marriages. Now arranged marriages are out of fashion. Men and women choose their own life partners, often outside their own community or religion. The practice of going abroad for education has brought many foreigners into orthodox Hindu families. Five-day marriages are unheard of. Completely overturning tradition and convention, the public reception for the married couple is held the day previous to the marriage ceremony and crowds disperse immediately after the wedding feast.

I was left in Aunt Kamalam's house for a month after my marriage to learn a little of Brahmin culture. Aunt Kamalam was my father's youngest sister. It used to be said of my paternal grandmother, Kalyani *Patti*, that she had so many children, she had to count them on her fingers. Kalyani *Patti* took her family responsibilities lightly. There is a story told of her selling ancestral land to buy peanuts. This may be a gross exaggeration, but she was spoken of as a carefree woman. Perhaps I got my scatterbrain genes from her!

My mother has told us that Kalyani *Patti* had eight daughters and two sons. My father's elder brother was Ramaswamy, named after his illustrious grandfather Elathur Ramaswamy Sastrigal, a great poet, who was compared to the poet Kalidasa and was given the name Kalidasa of the South. Unfortunately, most of his poetry was pawned or sold off by unworthy sons. His grandson Ramaswamy was no better. He was a compounder in Dr Narayana Iyer's clinic.

Dr Narayana Iyer was my eldest Aunt Chellamma's husband. He was an eminent surgeon and a contemporary of the famous Dr Rangachary, whose statue can be seen in Madras City. My uncle died when he was only 38 of a simple hernia surgery that his junior performed. My uncle must have performed hundreds of major operations successfully, and he died of a minor surgery! My father's elder brother Ramaswamy is said to have committed suicide. The circumstances that led him to this desperate step were hushed up, as it was a stigma on the family honour. He left behind a widow and four children. That branch of the family is not one to be proud of. None of the children made good in life. One of his granddaughters was Dharmambal, a popular announcer in the external services of All India Radio.

My grandmother's fifth daughter, Bhagavathy, is said to have eloped with a low-caste man. The family ostracized her. The elders in our family have always mentioned her in hushed tones, as if her very name would bring dishonour upon them. However, her elopement had a fairy-tale quality about it which we, as young girls found fascinating. I have only mentioned two skeletons from the family cupboard and do not intend to trace the history of my other aunts. The ones we knew and were in touch with were my Aunts Chellamma, Ammulu, Kittamma and Kamalam. Kittamma was married to a doctor and was in Rangoon. Aunts Kamalam and Ammulu served in the Ramana Ashram and died there.

My Aunt Kittamma is worth a special mention. During the Japanese bombing of Rangoon during World War II, thousands of refugees who could not find a place in the steamers walked all the way to India. Many died on the way. It was a question of survival of the fittest. The story goes that Aunt Kittamma, a strong and hefty woman, carried her husband most of the way since he was too weak to walk. Their children had left for India earlier with friends.

A month's stay in Aunt Kamalam's house in Karamanai, a village in Trivandrum, did not discipline me much. My aunt was the second wife of my Uncle Ayya, who was much older than she was. They had no children. My uncle was a primary teacher in a school and in his spare time he made ayurvedic *lehiyams* like *chavanprash, kushmanda lehiyam,* and other tonics. He was a nice old man and used to tell me stories from the *Puranas.* I remember his *Chandrahasa* and *Harishchandra* very well.

I had a friend next door, Anantalakshmi. She and I used to roam around, go to the Bhagavathy temple, play hopscotch with other girls for hours on end, and come home late in the evening. My aunt used to warn me to be careful about not losing my bangles or chain, and I used to saucily tell her: 'Here, Aunt! I have come back safe with my two eyes, two ears and hands and feet intact.' But soon I had to rue my impertinence. While playing an indoor game, I removed my gold wedding ring and lost it. I never found it again. That curbed my tongue—for a while.

In the month of Adi corresponding to the period between July 15 and August 15, girls of all ages danced the *Kummi* and *Kolattam,* which were like the *Dandia* of Gujarat. Each girl would have two wooden sticks, polished and coloured, two inches thick and a foot long. They would sing songs and swing the sticks to the beat of the music, striking the stick of the next girl with one hand. It was all a pattern and the steps were not easy, one had to practise the dance and strike in unison. All of us from Karamanai went to the Fort Padmanabha Swami Temple. Many girls would join us. *Kolattam* is now a dying art. It was a beautiful sight to see girls dressed in colourful long skirts and blouses dancing the *Kolattam.* Young married ladies also danced in villages.

A few years after I had lived with Aunt Kamalam, my uncle died. Aunt Kamalam went to live with her elder sister Ammulu in Tiruvannamalai. She spent the rest of her life in the Ramana Ashram. Being illiterate she knew nothing other than housework. She was such a simple soul and so lonely that she would talk to the cats and the dogs and even to the trees and plants. She lived and died in genteel poverty. The house was taken over by the Ashram after her death since Aunt Ammulu had bequeathed it to the Ashram.

My finishing school stay in acquiring Brahmanical culture came to an abrupt end, and I went back with my parents to Kandy. My husband came to Kandy on his first visit to his in-laws' house. I went with Daddy to the station to receive him. I was wearing a red Kanjeevaram silk sari. I remember this because he told me later that red suited me. I had rejoined school for the last term of the year. My husband and I used to go out for walks, and next day at school I would be asked by my friends, 'Who was that handsome chap, I say, with whom you were walking yesterday?' I would reply with studied casuality, 'Oh, he is my cousin from India,' as if he were nothing more than that. No one in my class knew that I was married or that I would have to leave school that December. Although married, my husband and I could not live together. We had to wait till I attained puberty, after which, our nuptials were celebrated, marking our formal entry into married life. Apart from our daily walks, Daddy would drop us at the theatre and pick us up at the end of the show. This way we saw quite a few English movies. In those days there were only two cinema halls in Kandy—the Empire and the Wembley. I was in my sixth standard in 1937, but did not complete the final term.

I have to now report an event, which came like a storm into our lives and created a lot of unpleasantness.

There was an Andhra gentleman Mr Subharaghavayya who was a frequent visitor to our house. He was a good astrologer, a good storyteller, in short, a very interesting person. After lunch or dinner he would sit surrounded by all the members of the family—except me and the other younger ones—and would regale them with stories. Mother would bring out the family horoscope book, and he would look into it and make predictions. We had a Mangalore Brahmin cook called

Shanbaghe. He would make hot chilly chutneys for
Subharaghavayya. Subharaghavayya had intervened when my
parents were hesitant to approach my uncle and aunt with
the proposal of my marriage to my cousin Ramaswamy.
He had strongly insisted that they go down on their knees
before them if necessary and somehow fix up the alliance, as
this was the only match for me. That was the only good deed
he did for our family. The man otherwise brought untold
suffering upon us.

Anantha and my eldest brother-in-law, Pamanji, were both
unemployed. Subharaghavayya talked my father and mother
into investing Rs 40,000 in an estate in Batticaloa. It was a 1500-
acre coconut estate with other crops as well. For giving them
this information and for his supervision of the estate along with
the two young men (my brother and brother-in-law), who
would be under him, he wanted a third of the share in the
property without contributing a cent.

For all the wisdom elders profess, I cannot understand how
and why my parents fell into such a trap. The deal went
through. And whenever it was necessary to make up a party
of four Brahmins while negotiations were going on, my
husband was included in them. It was considered inauspicious
for three Brahmins to start any venture, even going for a walk.
My husband used to recount with bitterness in later years how
he had been made use of as the fourth Brahmin, though my
parents did not think of making him a partner in the business.
But he had God's grace, as I would tell him, and that was why
he was not included in the venture.

The estate was purchased from a Chettiar, and it was agreed
that each of the three partners would stay in the estate for four
months to manage it. It did not take long for the true colours
of this Telugu Brahmin to start showing, leading to a lot of
misunderstanding and anger against him. He even threatened
to murder anyone who opposed him. A Sikh named Ganga
Singh was appointed as a security man. My husband narrated

to me how he was asked to spend the night with Subharaghavayya, a fearsome daredevil to those who were afraid of him. They said Subharaghavayya was not against my husband and would not harm him, but on the contrary had genuine affection for him.

How did all this trouble arise? Who was responsible for it? Could all the blame be laid on Subharaghavayya? I am not sure. Perhaps all this happeneed because my father distrusted him after having given him full powers—these are points I cannot clarify and those who could have explained the circumstances more clearly are no more.

The episode came to an end when a compromise was reached and Subharaghavayya was got rid off by paying him ten thousand rupees. Now Anantha and Pamanji were the owners of this vast property. I have stayed there and roamed around the place. The first owner was an Englishman, Sir Octerloney, who built a beautiful bungalow right on the seashore and a small house some distance away. The steps from the back verandah of the big house led straight to the sea. All of us stayed in the small house, as the big bungalow was frighteningly big and one did not feel safe there. And that was where my husband kept company with Subharaghavayya! There was a library full of books and I read my Rider Haggard, John Buchanan, and Wilkie Collins there.

Neither my brother nor my brother-in-law made a success of managing the vast property and, finally, it was sold at a loss to a Chettiar. That was the end of our ownership of Easter Seaton Estate, Batticaloa. But it was a fabulous estate, rich in not only coconuts but also paddy, mangoes, and bamboo forests. Everything that grew on that estate was money. The locals made baskets and beautiful items out of bamboo cane. Bee keeping was a flourishing business; snakes, which were in plenty, were killed and the skins sold. The local Tamils would light a lamp everyday and place a dish of milk as offering to the snakes so that they would not attack human beings. A kind of stunted shrub, which was said to be a snake repellent, was planted right round the house to keep off snakes. But my brother and brother-in-law had had enough of living with snakes and tackling the labourers, who were a troublesome lot. So they decided to quit. Perhaps the inauspicious trio of Brahmins entering into a partnership was responsible!

Soon after, my husband went to Madras and joined the *Madras Mail* (a leading evening daily), as an apprentice without a salary. He learnt journalism while gathering news in the police courts or while covering official functions and other important events in the city. The *Madras Mail* newsmen had to compete with *The Hindu*, an important morning daily. The reporting had to be handled in such a way that the news was not a repeat of *The Hindu* coverage. In those days graduates and postgraduates did not go in for journalism. There were two others with my husband who were also graduates like him. The editor of the *Madras Mail* was an Englishman, Mr Arthur Hayles. He liked Ramaswamy's work and offered him a permanent job on a salary of Rs 75. But Mr Ramaswamy, an M.A., would accept nothing less than Rs 150 and so quit the job in early 1937.

Goma's husband Mani came to Kandy for a visit and she was dancing attendance on him. Anantha and Saroja had come to stay, and the house was lively. Padha, Sarasa and Krishna's daughter Baby were going to school together. Baby's official name was Chellamma after her grandmother, but she was given the fashionable name Indira. I had stopped going to school. My educational qualification was first form, exam not taken. A Parsi lady, Miss Zorah, was appointed to teach me English, sewing, and general knowledge at home. She was very fair with bobbed hair and wore a frock. Anantha and Mani would wait to greet her with a 'Good afternoon, Miss.' We used to tease them about this, saying that this was their homage to white skin.

She dictated my reply to my husband's first letter to me. I remember one sentence: 'There is a picture palace nearby and they are now showing an English film called *The Garden of Allah*.' That was the only letter I wrote under her dictation. I used to get two to three letters a week and I replied as frequently. I think we really came to know each other through letters. I have a huge pile of letters we wrote to each other through the years. I attained puberty a year later and a telegram was sent to my in-laws. There were small functions in our house and in my in-laws' house.

Sister-in-law Thevoo Akka's daughter Padma was born some nine months after my marriage. Forty days after the child's birth, her father Iyya died suddenly in his village in Krishnapuram. Like her mother-in-law, Thevoo became a widow, that too when she was barely twenty-six.

Some say it was diphtheria, not detected; some say meningitis; anyway it was some fell disease that took away his life. Iyya hadn't even seen his newborn baby. On hearing the news, Mama rushed to Trivandrum. She was very fond of her brother's children. It was a tragedy that could be healed only with time. In those days losing one's husband and becoming a widow was hell's punishment among orthodox Brahmins. Poor Thevoo Akka went to Krishnapuram and stayed there with her infant daughter and two elder children, as her mother-in-law was alone and inconsolable. She had to stay inside the house and not show her unfortunate face to anyone. A year-long mourning with people coming in to condole and console would end by their rubbing salt on her wounds and making her cry bitterly for hours. They would paint a miserable future for her—at the mercy of her parents and brothers to whom she would have to turn for support. But fortunately for her, her family saw to it that she was not disfigured and gave her full support.

Thevoo Akka was a courageous lady, and her mother-in-law looked after her like a daughter and doted on her. Both mother-in-law and daughter-in-law vied with each other to make sacrifices. Her parents and brothers and sisters stood by her and though no one could help her in her grief, they all helped her overcome the pain and suffering. The grandmother and mother lived for the children.

My mother never wore her hair in braids after this tragedy; she would only tie it up in a knot. Time moved on.

A word about my Aunt Ammulu—short for Alamelu. She was a child widow, widowed at the age of seven, just four months after marriage. In those days even child widows were not spared the disfigurations of tonsure and the wearing of white for the rest of their lives. Widows had to go to the temple tank to have a bath before sunrise, before others could see them because their very sight was regarded as inauspicious. After four or five years they could come out and meet people, but their active participation was still not welcomed by society or their immediate family. For instance, if family members were negotiating for an auspicious event like an impending marriage and a widow walked in, they would suspend the discussion. So willy-nilly the widow would be forced to confine herself to the kitchen and her room.

Fortunately for my Aunt Ammulu, Aunt Chellamma's husband Dr Narayana Iyer was a strong personality. He forbade the tonsuring of her head and took her away with him to Salem. She stayed with her elder sister Chellamma and brother-in-law Dr Narayana Iyer. He engaged tutors to make her fit to take the SSLC Level examination. He wanted to put her in a hostel in Madras in Dr Muthulakshmi's school, but all the uncles from Trivandrum travelled all the way to Salem. They warned off Dr Narayana Iyer about daring to sending a widow to school, saying it would bring shame to the family. So Aunt Ammulu was educated at home. She used to do the cooking in the house and in the night would study by lantern light. She became a linguist. She knew Hindi, English, Bengali and Gujarati apart from the southern languages. She was a talented, courageous lady. Years later she built a small house in Tiruvannamalai and was interpreter to the foreigners as well as the Hindi, Gujarati, and Bengali devotees in the Ramana Ashram. She died in Tiruvannamalai at the age of seventy-five.

Baby (my niece Indira) and Sarasa (my youngest sister) were quite a pair, the latter being only six months older. They went to school together by rickshaw. They had observed Daddy occasionally stop the car for petrol when we went for a drive and get money back from the petrol pump owner. What they did not see was Daddy giving him a cheque against the cash. They thought one had only to ask the petrol man for money, whenever one needed some. The petrol pump was on the way to school. Quite often, Baby and Sarasa would ask the rickshaw man to go to the petrol pump and would go in and ask for five or ten rupees. The owner knew Daddy well and had seen both sitting in the car, so he gave them money whenever they wanted. It so happened that after a long time Daddy went in to fill petrol and cash a cheque at the same pump. The man gave Daddy a slip of paper on which he had entered the money taken by Baby and Sarasa. Daddy paid him and asked the kids what they had wanted the money for. They had mainly spent it on ice creams, fruit, and anything that was sold by the vendors outside the school gate. They were only six and five-and-a-half years old and they really thought it was all right to have done so!

We children (at twelve I was still a child, although I was married) enjoyed the drives to Kandy town. From Peradeniya Road to Kandy town was only four miles. The scenery one passed through was inexpressibly beautiful. One could see the contours of the hills all around. The road was wide and clean. After two miles the road skirted a shimmering blue lake, bordered on all sides by trees and flowering plants. We would sometimes stop the car and go down to the lake. The road beside the lake turned sharply to a steep and risky incline. Cars would climb round and round the mountain till one suddenly came upon a flat platform. Suddenly one stood before a huge park filled with a profusion of flowers, a riot of colours. The flowers were planted in small patches surrounded by stretches of green grass. Stone benches were liberally provided. I used to love Ves Park, as it was called, but never got over my fear of the steep climb.

After a year with the *Madras Mail* my husband joined Reuters, Colombo, on a salary of Rs 150, early in December 1937. A week later he asked his boss, Mr T.R.V. Chari, for a two-week leave. Our nuptials were fixed for 29 December 1937 in Trivandrum. Mr Chari being a South Indian Brahmin knew of the custom, but was reluctant to grant leave to a person who had joined only a week ago. However, he did sanction the leave and Daddy, my husband, and I travelled together to Trivandrum. Mama and others had gone on earlier. This was in a way our real marriage day. The function was celebrated on a grand scale with all relatives attending.

I was innocent and knew nothing about what marriage meant for a girl. My knowledge was confined to whisperings by classmates of having boy friends, hugging and kissing. In those days no one thought of sex education for children although child marriage was an established custom. On the contrary we were forbidden to mention sex or ask questions about it. The elders in the house studiously avoided all discussions on the topic.

Our nuptial chamber was decorated with flower garlands strung decorously from the double cots. Rose petals were strewn on the mattress and lighted incense gave off a heady fragrance. Earlier in the day, I was given a bath and dressed up in a grand silk sari. I was about to go to the hall to sit along with my husband for the Vedic rituals when—horror of horrors—I felt a wetness between my thighs. My periods had begun within a span of fifteen days. A woman at such times was regarded as being polluted and a polluting agent. She had, therefore, to stay segregated for three days, being allowed into the house only after her bath on the fourth day. What was I to do? I was trembling with fear. I confided in Goma. She advised me to keep mum and be absolutely normal. The household had incurred enormous expenses in arranging for the nuptials and a cancellation at this stage was impossible. I went through the rituals and in the night I was sent to my husband, who was waiting for me in the room. All the while the household women sang bawdy songs, full of innuendoes and suggestions. As advised by my sister, I feigned a headache and managed to ward off my husband. Next morning, I announced I had periods and was sent to an empty house to pass my three days of pollution. It was only on the third of January 1938 that we consummated our marriage.

For years I was haunted by the fear that I had polluted a Vedic ritual and was afraid of the consequences of sitting in front of the sacred fire during my menstrual cycle. My fears gradually went away, and I believe the gods abundantly blessed me because my husband and I were very happy and lived a glorious fifty-seven years together.

A week after this all of us left for Kandy. My husband rejoined his office in Colombo while I was in Kandy. The training my husband had in Reuters made him a seasoned newsman. He was on night duty for five years continuously. He would take the bus from Colombo on Saturday morning, after night duty, and arrive at Arifa House at 9 or 10 the next morning. This is how we started our weekend honeymoons.

On Monday morning he would leave for Colombo and I would be so miserable, I would just sleep away my loneliness for a day or two. My mother too was fond of her nephew and would talk for hours about their relatives in Trivandrum.

In 1939, Pandit Nehru visited Ceylon with his sister Mrs Krishna Huthee Singh. His visit was in an unofficial capacity as an important emissary from India. Though the visit had the tacit approval of the two British governments on either

side of Palk Straits, Mr Nehru was still under the surveillance
of British Intelligence. My husband was sent to cover the visit.
He and three other journalists from the local newspapers went
in a car driving ahead of Nehru's Humber, like a pilot car,
throughout his visit to Kandy and then on to the tea
plantations. The large crowds that gathered to greet him, the
poor estate labourers shouting 'Govinda, Govinda', as if God
had descended on them, overwhelmed Nehru.

The Sinhalese had a secret admiration for India and her
leaders. After the visit of Krishna Huthee Singh it became the
fashion for ladies of the upper crust to wear their saris the way
it was worn by Mrs Singh—the *pallu* would be brought across
the right shoulder and tucked in at the waist on the left side.
They also adopted the Krishna Huthee Singh haircut. As for
the men, the Nehru jackets came into vogue!

My sister Krishna's second daughter, Shanti, was born
in Arifa House in 1938. We had a family staying just opposite
our house. Mrs Ratnaswami was a widow with three daughters
and a son. We were very good friends. Mama asked her to
stay in our house when Krishna went into labour. Mrs
Ratnaswami helped during Goma's and my delivery. Mrs
Ratnaswami's eldest daughter, Rosy, was a straight-laced
woman. She was the boss in the house and Mrs Ratnaswami
was proud of her (or perhaps scared) and would refer to her
as 'My Rosy.' It was common for us to hear 'My Rosy said
this, my Rosy said that'. In our family we jokingly referred to
anyone who was boasting as 'My Rosy.' Goma's first daughter
Leela was born in 1939.

My first child, a daughter, was born on 25 May 1940. We
named her Kalyani after my husband's mother. A Tamil
woman from one of the tea estates, reputed to be a good
midwife, came to stay with us for a week before the baby was
due and stayed on for another week after the delivery. Our
family doctor Dr Sreenivasan was also present. I was only
fifteen. I remember being terrified by the pregnancy and the

impending delivery, even thinking at times that I would not survive the ordeal. I recall looking out of the window of my room, tears streaming down my face, bidding farewell to the familiar world around me. In those days most deliveries were done in the house, since no one went to the hospital. Deliveries were mostly left in the competent hands of midwives. It was not uncommon for women to die during childbirth.

My baby was born at 6.37 p.m., and Daddy informed my husband on the phone. The proud father reached Kandy at midnight to see the first-born. We were very happy parents and decided to have a large family, but never visualised a single-gender series of six. My father-in-law came all the way from Trivandrum to see his granddaughter. As my two elder sisters-in-law had each a daughter named Kalyani, my daughter was called Kunju (meaning 'little') Kalyani. 'Kalyani' was eventually dropped and everyone called her Kunju. Three years later, after we had left Ceylon forever and I was with my mother in Salem, a ladies' club friend of mine, Mrs Rajaram, changed her name from Kunju to Manju. The name Manju stuck.

Manju was six months old when we left Kandy. I went to Trivandrum to stay with my in-laws. Mama went to Salem; she was building a house there. Anantha and Saroja were also in Salem. My father was in Kandy. My husband's younger brother Mani had also taken up a job in Colombo in 1939. He had just finished his history honours examination and the results had not yet come. The Chief of the Chamber of Commerce in Colombo was one Mr Rajagopala Iyer. He was looking for a young assistant. My husband wrote out an application, signed it on behalf of his brother, and gave it to Mr Rajagopala Iyer. Mr Iyer was willing to appoint Mani, but mentioned that he would like to see the candidate in person before issuing the appointment. My husband told him, 'Sir, he looks very much like me, only fairer in complexion.' Mr Iyer must have been impressed with my husband's personality because he gave instructions for the appointment letter to be sent to Mani. Mani soon joined the Chamber of Commerce, Colombo.

Another member of our family also took up a job in Colombo. My mother's younger brother R. Padmanabhan joined the Indian Bank in Colombo. Though a half brother, he and his three sisters were close to our family. My Aunt Chellamma, her son Chandran—about ten years old—and a daughter, Kokila, came to Kandy and stayed with us for a few days before going to Colombo to join uncle.

As the names of cowboys of the Wild West in America take a prefix, so did Indian names of those who were either settled or employed in Colombo. It was in a rented portion of 'Gunboat' Ramaswami's house that my uncle's family stayed. Then there was the family I have mentioned earlier, 'Sunlight' Shankara Iyer, and my husband's friend 'Paramount' Krishna Iyer, who was employed in Paramount Pictures. If you knew the man's name, you knew where he was employed!

I went with Daddy to Colombo when he went on official trips. My husband showed me the room in Adamally Buildings where he stayed with his brother Mani and two other friends, Mr Govinda Iyer and Parameswaran. Their food was brought in tiffin carriers to the room. He also took me to his office; we had the room to ourselves as the staff had gone out for lunch. The office was on the fourth or fifth floor—I am not sure—but I remember we could see the busy thoroughfare down in the street and had a view of Colombo City. We spent the night in V.S. Rao's house.

My husband regaled me with stories of his roommates in Adamally Buildings. Paramesvaran or Pammeechan, as they called him, was a Keralite. Once he received a container of pure home-made ghee sent by his parents. But, the poor chap went down with fever and waited for a week to savour the ghee. The fever persisted even as roommates consumed the ghee, never failing to comment upon its excellence. At last he could not withstand the temptation. When the others were out of the room, he finished all the ghee. On their return the anxious roommates observed Pammeechan for any ill-effects but found none. From then on Pammeechan became *"neiy* (Tamil for ghee) Pammeechan.'

Another time my husband, who always considered himself a good cook (though I never saw any evidence of it), invited his friend Paramount Krishna Iyer for tea. They decided to make *rawa* (semolina) halwa. The *rawa* was added to sugar syrup and allowed to thicken without being first fried and cooked in water. What they made must have been an awfully gluey dish. They put in generous dollops of ghee and the poor guest, Krishna Iyer, had generous helpings of it. It was only later that they realized the frightful mistake they had committed in not cooking the *rawa* before adding the sugar. They were horrified at the thought of the damage the halwa might do to the unfortunate Mr Krishna Iyer. Luckily for them, except for complaining of a severe stomach ache, Krishna Iyer survived.

On one of my visits to Colombo, I also visited Uncle Padmanabhan. I thought Aunt Chellamma was beautiful. Chandran was quite a precocious child. He would discuss politics and was a bright lad. After August 1939, I did not visit Colombo.

My eldest daughter Manju and my aunt's daughter Vasantha were born in the same month. Aunt Chellamma went home to Puliyur, a village in Trivandrum district, for her delivery. We were all grieved to hear about the sudden and tragic death of her first daughter Kokila; she had also lost a son Natarajan before coming to Ceylon. I don't think she came back to Ceylon after Vasantha was born. Uncle went back to Alleppey. My mother left for Salem, and I went to stay in Taikad, Trivandrum, with my in-laws.

Manju was six months old. She was an attractive baby. I felt clumsy and awkward carrying her. I used to carry her on my hip and whenever I went through a doorway I would knock her head against the doorframe. I was just sixteen and too young to be a mother.

Sethu as a bride, Trivandrum 1935.

Sethu at 14, Kandy.

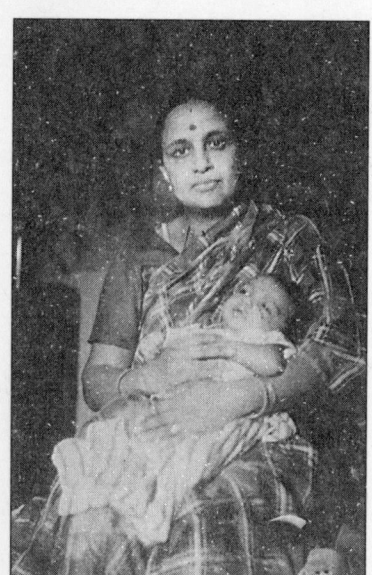

Sethu at 15, with her first-born, Manju.

Sethu as a grandmother and great grandmother, Delhi 2002.

Sehu´s parents with her only brother Anantha, Batticaloa 1936.

Setnu s parents, Anandammal and A.S. Narayanan, Trivandrum 1913.

Sethu´s father-in-law, R. Padmanabha Iyer, Trivandrum 1935.

Sethu's husband, P. Ramaswamy, New Delhi 1953.

II

TRIVANDRUM

My Life In Taikad

❧

My in-laws' household was orthodox, well ordered, and disciplined. It was a large family. My widowed sister-in-law, Thevoo, lived there with her youngest and eldest daughters, Padma and Kalyani respectively, and son Shankaran. Another sister-in-law Sarojem was there and also Ambujam and Lakshmanan and Sundaram, the two younger boys, and Sarada, the youngest at six years. My father-in-law was *anchal* (postal) Superintendent for the whole of Travancore and had to do a lot of touring to inspect the district post offices. There were three peons, all Brahmins, attached to the house. One was employed as a cook and the other two in a general capacity. Other clerks and peons would frequently come to the house. They would help in outdoor work. There were two peons and, by some strange chance, both had the same name: Rajangam Iyer. One was called Senior R and the other, Junior R. The cook was Sreenivasan Pothi. *Pothis* are Mangalore Brahmins. They were either priests in a temple or cooks. A few, like our

Sreenivasan Pothi, broke away from tradition and came to work for the government. But even here Pothi had to work as a cook. Before my father-in-law retired, he promoted many of these people to clerks and assistant postmasters.

The entire house was under the control of my mother-in-law. She was a majestic figure, very fair—I would say almost white—and very serious. I had just read Tagore's *Gora* and began to weave a fantasy. My mother-in-law's complexion intrigued me, and I wondered if someone up the ancestral tree had strayed? She was rigid in her orthodoxy. I wondered what would happen if like Gora she were to suddenly discover that she was not a pure Brahmin, but one polluted by foreign blood!

I was not conversant with the rules of orthodoxy and would make mistakes. There were so many rules that unless one had been trained in such a household since childhood, it was difficult to know the dos and don'ts. For instance, while eating meals sitting on the floor either from plantain leaves or brass plates, if the serving ladle happened to touch the plate or leaf of the person who was eating, the entire contents of the serving dish would have to be thrown away. This notion of pollution in food is called *echchil* in Tamil. It is known as *jhootan* in Hindi, but there is no equivalent term in English since the concept itself is alien to them. In an extended sense, if while eating, one's garment happens to touch the plate, one would have to have a bath, as the whole body becomes *echchil.* These rules still prevail in some orthodox households, but are changing fast. My own grandchildren do not know what *echchil* is, let alone observing it in one's food habits.

At home, Sarojem, Ambujam, and I had nothing to do the whole day. Our only job was giving oil baths to the three boys and Sarada. On Saturday, the males of the house took an oil bath. A huge pot of water would be placed on the fire in the bathroom. The boys, the front of their heads shaven and with pigtails, would be anointed with oil on the head and body. The oil would be washed off with soapnut powder.

The oil bath was a must in every South Indian Brahmin household and detested the most by children. I remember I was given oil by my mother and asked to rub some into my head and smear some all over my body. I would do neither, but would quietly empty all the oil down the drain. When asked if I had applied oil properly and had a good bath, I would answer with a nod of the head since I was honest enough not to utter a lie. I quite sympathized with the boys when they grimaced and tried to put off the oil bath by making some excuse. But under the severe discipline of my mother-in-law there was no letting off. Sundaram and Shankaran would come like sacrificial goats and have the unpleasant job finished for them quickly, but Lakshman who was a playful boy, would run around and hide. When caught, he would be off again before one could bend down to smear his head with a handful of oil. Only when we would threaten to report his antics to higher authority, would he sit still while we poured the oil on his head. The children were marched off to the bathroom and after we had washed their heads with soapnut powder to take away the oil, they would be left to complete the bath.

The girls' other job was giving them their breakfast, which was yesterday's rice soaked in water and whatever curry was left over. There was a separate room for this and a separate corner in which the rice pot was kept, since old rice was again considered a 'pollutant' and castigated as *paththu*. *Paththu* can be described as a sister concept of *echchil*. Whatever is cooked becomes *paththu* and one has to cleanse one's fingers with water if one has touched it. Yesterday's food was not eaten by the orthodox elders. The old rice was mixed in curd or buttermilk with a little salt and the kids would sit round in a circle and one mouthful would be put in each one's palm. With the thumb they would make a dent and the curry would be poured in. After ten or fifteen rounds of rice, they would have their fill, and we girls could have our share. Only the elders took coffee and tea. Sometimes we had tea in the afternoons.

Pothi's cooking used to be excellent, consisting of jackfruit curry and all kinds of spicy dishes. My mouth waters to think of those delicious meals. With such a large family to provide for, the income was not adequate. But my mother-in-law somehow kept the house going by judicious management, providing plenty of food for everybody three times a day. Milk was scarce in Trivandrum and there were babies to be fed. Since I had grown up on milk, I used to get upset and cry to myself that I was denied milk. I even thought my mother-in-law was ill-treating me! At that time I did not realize what a tightrope walk managing the finances must have been. Every night my mother-in-law would sit in front of the storeroom—a small dark windowless room—and write the day's account. If I had taken a page out of my mother-in-law's account book and read it out to my grandchildren, it would have astonished them. For two rupees one could buy 25 kilos of rice. Two or three *chakrams* was the price of one litre of *gingelly* oil, coconut oil was even cheaper and groundnut and sunflower oils were not known. For lighting lamps, a cheap oil called *pinakku* was used. A kind of powdered jaggery was used for coffee and tea, white refined sugar being far too expensive at a couple of *chakrams* for a *raathal* (roughly equivalent to a pound). I must mention that the State of Travancore had its own currency—*kasu*, *chakram*, *panam*, and the rupee.

After writing the daily accounts, my mother-in-law would leisurely chew betel leaves rubbed with lime, adding betel nuts, two or three leaves rolled in one. That was the only time she was relaxed. Sarojem, Ambujam, little Sarada, and sister Thevoo would sit around and talk and my mother-in-law relaxed so much as to laugh a little. I would sit some distance away. It was an unwritten code that the daughter-in-law should not sit in front of the elders of the house, and whenever my in-laws entered a room where I was sitting, I had to stand up, even though they were my uncle and aunt. These were considered becoming and modest qualities in a daughter-in-law.

Sarojem and Ambujam did some sewing and embroidery and learnt *veena* from sister Thevoo. They were much advanced in their music and played *Kirtanams* (songs). I knew only how to strum film tunes and had not been taught the correct method. Sister Thevoo showed me how to play the scales and a few songs. Ambujam had a teacher for vocal music. There again as the daughter-in-law I could not learn music from a man. But thinking back, I feel that paying fees for two students must have been too much. That is why I was not asked to learn along with Ambujam. I must add that though I kept within the discipline imposed on the daughter-in-law of the house, I was treated just like a daughter and found a lot of love. I used to listen and learn the songs the teacher taught Ambujam.

In the front verandah of the house grandfather Kunjaman Appa (my mother-in-law's father) sat on a cot. He was blind. He had developed a cataract, which he refused to get removed because of his fear of being operated upon. So he remained blind for the rest of his life. He was a character from the *Puranas*, a man who lost his wife at the young age of twenty one and never married again. His infant daughter, the only offspring of the marriage, was three months old when his wife died. Her maternal grandmother brought up the motherless child.

The child's grandfather, Lakshmana Iyer, was a *tehsildar* and had some feudal powers. He had a large establishment and a fairly large family, but they said he had a roving eye. One known affair was with a Nair woman, a teacher in a primary school. This made his wife unhappy. People also said that when his wife complained of this to my maternal grandfather, Director of Education in Travancore, he immediately had the teacher transferred to a remote place.

There was another concubine of grandfather Lakshmana Iyer: a Nair woman named Kochchappi. A few months after I came to live in my in-laws' house, she made an appearance. A tall, gaunt old lady, she walked into our house from the rear entrance. She was asked to sit in the inner quadrangle and was given something to eat and drink. My sisters-in-law were muttering among themselves, 'Oh, the great grandmother has come claiming relationship. What does she think?' I hesitatingly asked them who she was and was told she was the keep of their maternal great grandfather. I looked at her with great curiosity, trying to trace the beauty that must have been there in her youth. I was introduced to her as '*kochchu swami inda bharya*' meaning 'the young master's wife.' She closed her fists, waved her knuckles around my head and cracked them at the two ends of her forehead—to ward off evil eyes. Even today, elderly south Indian ladies, among the Brahmins and the non-Brahmins, make the gesture for the protection of their loved ones. She took my baby in her lap and played with her. My mother-in-law came and talked to her for some time. They spoke in Malayalam, which I did not understand. She was given money, a measure of rice, betel leaves, and betel nuts. She went away happy.

When my mother-in-law was ten years old, she went to keep house for her father. Before that she stayed with her uncles (father's brothers), but was not happy with the aunts. Her marriage to my father-in-law was settled when she was in the cradle, so to say. My father-in-law's grandmother Annamma was Kunjaman Appa's elder sister. So she settled that the baby Kalyani would be the bride for her grandson Padmanabha. The reason why I am keen on relating this is that this motherless infant of three months lived to plant a family tree with many branches, more than one hundred, of whom, among others, my grandchildren are the offshoots.

Coming back to Kunjaman Appa, one would have to describe how he would walk through to the inner quadrangle of the house, sit in a particular place, and cut vegetables for lunch—without being able to see. He would ask some child or other to sit near him to tell him if the vegetables, like brinjals and snake gourd, were worm-eaten. Sitting on his cot in the front verandah he would know if a person had entered the house, come he ever so softly. He would shout, 'Who is there?' and would want to know the name of the person, who he was, and what he wanted. My father-in-law and even the boys would be annoyed at this cross-examination of their visitors. But Kunjaman Appa was an autocratic, stubborn old man.

In his village in Ashramam, he made his money by lending money on interest. He had paddy lands and derived his income from them. It was said of him that he never got a promissory note signed nor kept any written record of his lending. Everything worked on trust and, I am sure, such was the integrity of the village folk that he never lost or was cheated on a single transaction. Even Englishmen would come to him for loans. He was able to give his daughter gifts of jewellery whenever he visited them at their in-laws' house.

Ashramam, the village where my husband was born, has a place in Puranic mythology. Legend has it that Atri Maharishi and his wife Anusuya had their hermitage here. Anusuya is one of the *Pancha Kanya Satis* (five chaste wives). It is (or was) customary to say the names of these five *satis* every morning so that merit accrues to the housewife. The verse is as follows: *Anusuya, Draupadi, Sita, Tara, Mandodari tatha/Panchakanyam smarennityam sarva papa vinashanam.* It means: Anusuya, Draupadi, Sita, Tara and Mandodari/By remembering these five women, all sins are destroyed.

A story illustrates how a chaste woman is believed to be more powerful than the gods. Once Shiva, Vishnu, and Brahma came to test Sati Anusuya before her hermitage as three Brahmin mendicants and asked for food. They came when Atri Maharishi was away. It was the sacred duty of a *patni* (housewife) to feed Brahmins. Anusuya invited them to be seated while she prepared the food. The gods in disguise said they would take food only if it was served by the person in the nude. Anusuya, being a *sati*, had powers equal to that of the gods. She changed the gods by her *karpu* (spiritual power acquired through chastity) to three infants and fed them milk as per the stipulated condition. The consorts of the three gods—Parvati, Lakshmi, and Saraswati—came in search of their husbands and were aghast at finding them sleeping peacefully in their cradles. They begged Anusuya to restore their husbands to them. Anusuya did so. The mighty gods were put to shame and went away blessing her and acknowledging her greatness. This is how the place came to be called Ashramam.

My husband, his two elder sisters and four younger siblings were born in Ashramam. In those days, conditions for delivering a child were primitive. The small room in which grain was stored was converted into a labour room. There was no window or ventilator whatsoever. A thick curtain was put on the door and that was the only means by which air or light could enter. If it was night, only a chimney lamp or hurricane lantern was used for the midwife to deliver the baby. The midwife was often the barber's wife, usually untrained and sometimes assisted by an old and supposedly experienced Brahmin widow. Only the strong and sturdy women survived the delivery if anything went wrong. Nobody ever thought of having a male doctor attending on a delivery. Unless there was a crisis, a doctor—the nearest would be twelve miles away—would not be called. There were no women doctors; most women did not even have access to primary education.

The village women were hardy folks. One such lady, who happened to be an aunt of my father, was not only hardy, but also a daredevil. Valliammai Chithi, as she was called, had a quarrel with her mother-in-law and, angry, decided not to ask for help during her delivery. She bolted the front door, delivered her baby, cut the umbilical cord, delivered the placenta, and after dressing opened the front door. I am sure her mother-in-law would have been speechless. It was the talk of the village for a long time and still is. It must be a rare case in medical history, too.

Kunjaman Appa was exacting in his wants. He would take just less than half a tumbler of coffee, made just the way he wanted. A minute difference in quantity would make him furious and he would refuse to take coffee for a week in protest. His food would have to be served to him exactly as he wanted. One person was allotted the duty of attending on him. He had his favourites; sometimes it was Sarojem, sometimes Ambujam, sometimes me. Sister Thevoo was dearest to him, since she bore his wife's name, Devaki. In those days men too did not address their wives by name. He used to call sister by the pet name Ammakodam ('honey pot').

Appa was a past master in sarcasm. His brother's son, Suppu *mama*, an overseer, would sometimes visit us. Appa was prejudiced against him. Suppu *mama* would greet Appa first and then go inside to chat with his cousins and my in-laws. Appa from the front verandah would start a soliloquy that went like this: 'I have built palaces, temples, big buildings, I am a big engineer…' It was directed towards poor Suppu *mama* who may have been giving himself the airs of an architect. If someone asked him whom he was referring to, he would reply, 'Myself.' Appa had four brothers and between the five brothers there were only two progeny. Suppu *mama* was the son of his elder brother, and Appa had one daughter. Suppu *mama* had four daughters and two sons. He was poor and could hardly support his family. The little piece of land that he had, he sold for conducting the marriage of his daughters.

Appa's sarcasm was not confined to Suppu *mama*; any visitor who came to see his son-in-law was given a dose. Yet Appa was an embodiment of love with a rough exterior; all his caustic comments came out of his love for banter. He was afraid his son-in-law was gullible and would be imposed upon. The boys would sometimes have their friends visiting them and even if they were to tread ever so softly, Appa's keen ears would catch the sound and he would end up embarrassing the boys by conversing with their friends. He loved his grandchildren deeply, and when my husband or Mani came on leave and went back to Colombo he would be upset and shed tears.

My father-in-law had a lot of touring to do. Sometimes my mother-in-law accompanied him, and they also took a cook along. I went with them on a couple of trips. We would get VIP treatment in the guest houses and in the temples we visited. The priest would have the *aarti* specially done for us and give us garlands of jasmine flowers as *prasad*. We went to Ethmanoor, Vaikom and many other places and temples.

The temples of Kerala were different from those of Tamil Nadu. One could not enter a temple in Kerala without having a bath. The men were not allowed to wear shirts, they had to enter bare-bodied. Non-Hindus were not allowed inside a temple. The priests were the high upper-caste Namboodari Brahmins, called *Pothi*. They kept their distance from people and would throw the *prasad*, sandal paste on a piece of plantain leaf, into the outstretched palms of the devotees, since as I have already mentioned, touching caused pollution. I remember a Minister of Tamil Nadu who was given *prasad* by the priest in the usual manner. The Minister felt offended and insulted, and threatened to go to court saying the event smacked of caste discrimination. The temple authorities pacified him and assured him that it was the practice of the priest and even Brahmins received *prasad* that way.

Trivandrum, the capital of Travancore, is a beautiful city. The natural beach there is called *Shankumugam* (meaning Mouth of a Sea Shell). The houses in the city are picturesquely situated on hills and vales. Since the city has two or three rainy seasons in a year, an umbrella is part and parcel of everyone's attire. The men invariably wear their dhotis or *mundus* folded up to the waist.

The Kerala women are beautiful, with long hair reaching down to the knees, and eyes darkened with *kajal*, a natural black substance used as an eyeliner. Nowadays the women have taken to wearing saris, but then women wore *settu mundu*, the *mundu* (dhoti) with an upper cloth, absolutely white or off white, and a blouse. I once saw a Nair lady sitting on a chair and drying her long hair on the clothesline which, if let down, would have swept the floor. Kerala is also known for its unique folk traditions of dance such as *Kathakali* and *Ottamtullal.*

The history of Kerala is of personal interest to me. One of our ancestors, Rama Iyen, called Rama Iyen Dalawa (the suffix Dalawa refers to a Commander-in-chief) was Minister to Martanda Verma, the Maharaja of Travancore. Travancore was the site of one of the oldest kingdoms in the South. Folk belief is that its origin goes back to the beginning of the world. The Chera dynasty had ruled over this region during the Sangam age, that is, in the pre-Christian era. The region continued to form a part of Chera Nadu even during medieval times. The territory was a part of Dravida Desam or Tamilaham till the ninth century; Tamil was the language of the region. It was only around the ninth century that one begins to hear of Malayalam, which grew out of the Grantham script that in turn had alphabets with both Tamil and Sanskrit characters. Even today most literate old people from Kerala can fluently read the Grantham script, now confined to the exclusive use of the priestly class.

Long ago the southern region was divided into three kingdoms—Chera, Chola, and Pandya Nadu—governed by three different dynasties. It is said that Parasurama, the son of Rishi Jamadagni and one of the ten incarnations of Lord Vishnu, threw his axe from Cape Comorin and it fell at Gokarnam. Whereupon the sea receded from these two points to the present extent of the Malabar Coast, and he called it Keralam, or the Land of Coconuts. During the colonial period, the region became the kingdom of Travancore.

There have been some distinguished rulers of Travancore. Kulasekhara Perumal, the great Vaishnava saint and poet, ruled for some years and then abdicated to become a Vaishnava ascetic. He became a renowned Alwar saint. In the long line of rulers, Marthanda Verma stands out. With his able Dalawa, Rama Iyen, he brought about many reforms in the state. It was during his reign that the Maharajah laid his sword on the *Ottakal Mandapam* (a structure resting on a platform carved out of a single stone) in the presence of Sri Padmanabha Swamy, the chief deity of Travancore, and made over the kingdom to the temple. The king declared that from that moment he became the faithful servant of the deity, literally *Padmanabha Dasa,* and that he would conduct all affairs of the State as a trustee of God. This unique act was carried out on the advice of his Brahmin minister, Rama Iyen Dalawa. It was a strategy to save the state of Travancore from being absorbed by the British crown under the Doctrine of Lapse propounded by Lord Dalhousie. Under this doctrine, any State could lapse to the British crown if it did not have a direct heir to the throne or if the State was being misgoverned. When the British Agent confronted Travancore with the Doctrine, the king claimed that it could not apply to this State as all the Maharajas ruled in the name of Sri Padmanabha Swamy and as such bore the title *Padmanabha Dasa.* So it was not the Maharaja's heir who ascended the throne but the 'heir' of Sri Padmanabha Swamy. This celebrated incident is narrated with particular pride within our family circles because our ancestor Rama Iyen Dalawa had provided a remarkable solution to a grave political crisis.

I have been told that this illustrious ancestor of mine, Rama Iyen, was a poor Brahmin boy who, by virtue of his intelligence and genius, rose to the highest offices in the State, becoming both Prime Minister and Commander-in-Chief of Travancore. As a young boy, his father, who was one of the chief priests of the king, brought him to the court of Travancore. A worship was taking place and the young Rama Iyen was keenly observing the proceedings. He noticed that the light in one of the lamps was flickering and becoming dim. If the lamp went out, he knew, it would be considered an ill-omen. Rama Iyen quietly got up, took a cotton wick, dipped it in oil and placed it in the lamp, which began to burn brightly once again. The Maharaja watched the action of the little boy with keen interest. After the worship, he requested the father to leave the boy in his care. He was brought up in the palace and given high education. In course of time Rama Iyen proved himself worthy of the king's love and confidence. With his brilliant intellect he could provide quick solutions to many vexing political problems.

In his political astuteness Rama Iyen Dalawa has often been compared to Chanakya, the legendary Prime Minister of Chandragupta Maurya and the author of the first Indian treatise on political theory, the *Arthashastra*. He is credited with introducing a rate list for all essential commodities, especially food products, thereby standardising prices and preventing black marketing and its corollary, inflation. The man was so meticulous that like a careful housewife, he is said to have maintained a table giving the measurements of rice, pulses and other commodities and their prevalent prices.

The Dalawa was in the process of repairing and constructing better defences within the palace fort when he fell fatally ill. The king sent his nephew Balarama Verma, the 'Ilaya Raja', to the ailing minister at Mavelikkera. When the prince enquired of him what his last wishes were, the only regret Rama Iyen Dalawa expressed was that he had failed to succeed in his mission to annex Cochin to the State of Travancore. He had nothing to ask for himself since he was a servant of the Maharaja. Rama Iyen Dalawa never married. We are actually the descendants of his brother's line. It is ironic that no one in our family has entered military service despite having descended from the great Commander-in-Chief.

Similarly, no account of Travancore can afford to leave out the legendary Svati Tirunal. In 1829, His Highness Maharaja Rama Verma ascended the throne at the age of sixteen. He had been born under the constellation Svati and therefore came to be called 'Svati Tirunal.' Apart from being a wise and able administrator, he was a great scholar and had mastered several languages, which included English, Sanskrit, Persian, Hindi, and

Marathi apart from the languages of the south. He composed songs in Malayalam, Telugu, Sanskrit, and Hindi. He was a contemporary of the trinity of classical music—Thyagaraja, Shyama Shastri, and Muthuswami Dikshitar.

I am reminded of a popular story, which forms part of our musical lore. It is said that Svati Tirunal sent his court musician Govinda Marar as an emissary to Thyagaraja to invite him to the court of Travancore. When the two met, Marar sang a rendering in Raga Arabi in the course of an evening musical session. This impressed Thyagaraja so much that he composed the famous kirtanam 'Entharo Mahanubhavulu, antharikki vandanamulu' meaning 'To the many great musicians, my salutations.' Thyagaraja, however, firmly refused to attend upon any king, however great.

To return to the present: Sarojem, Ambujam, and I were close friends. Our only outings were occasional visits to nearby temples. On Tuesdays, we would go to the Subramanya Swami temple and on Saturdays, to the Sastha temple, each god having a special day. There were annual festivals in the Padmanabha Swamy temple and in the Fort. We would go by car to see the Arattu procession from Krishna mama's house in East Fort Street.

In front of the main sanctum sanctorum of Sri Padmanabha Swamy, where the statue lies in a reclining pose and covers three doorways (one opening at the head, one in the middle and one at the foot), a platform is carved out of a single stone, Ottakal Mandapam. No one was allowed to prostrate himself on that platform, only the Maharaja who ruled in the name of Lord Padmanabha Swamy could do so.

In front of that platform there is a place where my maternal grandfather P. Ramaswamy Iyer prostrated himself full length during nirmalya darshan (which was at 3 a.m.) every day for thirty five years. Nirmalya darshan occurred when the doors of the sanctum sanctorum were thrown open at 3 in the morning, and devotees could see the Lord in all his glory as

He was the previous night. It was believed He was most beneficent at this time.

My grandfather was quite literally a towering figure, he stood a little above six feet. He was perhaps the first graduate in the community and held a high position in Travancore State. Like his father and grandfather before him, he was also close to the palace. He was Deputy Director of Education for the whole of Travancore and coined the slogan, 'A school a mile.' He was responsible for laying the foundation of today's high percentage of literacy in Kerala. There are also many stories of his blatant nepotism in appointing relatives as teachers in these schools. Being the first person in the family to occupy a high position and having a large number of hangers-on within the family, he was under tremendous pressure from his respected aunts and uncles to give employment to his numerous nephews and cousins.

The Director of Education was an Englishman, Dr Mitchell. My grandfather had many enemies who were jealous of his position, and some of them carried tales to Dr Mitchell that the schools were not functioning and that the teachers were idle. Dr Mitchell announced the closure of some schools in Kanyakumari district. When grandfather came home that evening he found all the primary teachers of that district, most of them his relatives, in the house. The elders raised a hue and cry that the nephews and cousins would all now starve without a job if Chamy (short for Ramaswamy) did not do something to save them. Grandfather shut himself up in his room and planned a strategy. He visited the villages where the schools were located, called the people—mostly poor' Muslims who had no interest in sending their children to school—and told them that the *Dorai*, as an Englishman was referred to, would be visiting their village. He told them that if they wanted better amenities for water they should all raise their hands when the *Dorai* asked them what they wanted.

His next step was to see Dr Mitchell and convince him that the people in the villages wanted their children to go to school. They were angry and disappointed at the closure of the schools and that Dr Mitchell could verify this by going to the villages and asking them directly.

Poor Mitchell did not know a word of Malayalam. When he went to the villages, he asked the villagers if they wanted to send their children to school. (My grandfather naturally translated the question as: 'The *Dorai* is asking you if you need more wells to be bored for water.') All hands were raised and a cry of 'Aye' went up. Dr Mitchell was more than convinced and promptly issued orders to reopen the schools. The primary school teachers were reinstated, and his uncles and aunts blessed grandfather.

Once a year the director made visits to inspect the schools. The English teacher of the primary school in Kanyakumari was a nephew of grandfather. As soon as he got prior intimation of the impending inspection visit he swung into action and launched 'Operation Inspection.'

He took home the English textbook of every student, chose a lesson, folded the page there and put a weight on it. Thus all the 20 or 30 books were folded at the same page. If one were to casually open any book for a random selection it would open only at that page. While the pages were being set at home, he drilled the children with questions and answers from that particular lesson till they could answer any question even in their sleep. This was the only teaching he did the entire year, his school time being spent in more useful pursuits like card games, and a kind of country chess, besides chewing betel leaf and having restful naps.

The great day arrived. All the textbooks had been distributed to their owners just a day before.

The director came accompanied by my grandfather. The teacher was introduced to him and Dr Mitchell casually picked up a textbook from the third row of benches. It was understood that the front benches had good students. The page opened out exactly as planned, and the director fired several questions from the lesson to the students picking out boys from here and there. For every question asked, pat came the answer. Here I must add that English was introduced right in the lower class. The Maharaja was particular that English should be taught early in school.

The director was immensely pleased and patted the teacher on his back. He had to leave in a hurry and could not spend more than a few minutes in this class. The teacher heaved a great sigh of relief and lashing the desk with a few strokes of his cane to keep the students quiet, he relaxed with a cup of coffee from the flask thoughtfully brought from home.

Meanwhile, Grandfather excused himself from going back with the director with the plea of having some personal work to do. After seeing the director off, he came again to the class of the English teacher. He went to each desk, opening out the English textbook, and just as he suspected he found all the books opening at the same page. He dismissed the class and gave his nephew a tongue-lashing and put the fear of God in him, warning him of never resorting to such tricks. But a seasoned bandicoot is a seasoned bandicoot, and the effects of the severe talking to must have soon worn off.

Grandfather's strategy may not have been honourable or strictly in keeping with the codes of conduct and honesty, but many things were got around in those days of intrigue through wit. And I am sure truant teachers and students alike learnt a lesson. There were many instances of grandfather having to manoeuvre through difficult situations. Serving royal masters was not an easy task. Grandfather died soon after retirement at the age of fifty-nine, having married twice. He left behind a contingent of family members supported and maintained by him. So ended an era.

It is not always possible for a family to trace their ancestors very far back. This is possible only among royalty and that too, only where the dynasty has had continuity. My maternal grandfather, his father, and grandfather were well-known scions of the family. All of them served the Maharaja and moved freely in the palace.

There is a painting of my great grandfather R. Padmanabha Iyer (referred to by everyone as Pappu Anna), by the famous Kerala painter Prince Ravi Verma, who was his friend. He is shown as he looked after a visit to the temple, his right hand holding the temple *prasad*, half a coconut with sandal paste and *tulsi* leaves. He is shown with marks of sandalwood paste on his bare chest and arms and wearing a chain of *rudraksha* and gold beads, each one as big as a gooseberry. This family heirloom is still with us. The gold beads alone would fetch a fortune.

The father of R. Padmanabha Iyer was Rama Iyer. He earned the name of 'Adamangai' Rama Iyer for the service he rendered to the Maharani. The story goes that once the Maharani had a severe stomach disorder; perhaps it would have been diagnosed as dysentery or gastroenteritis these days.

The palace *Vaids* could not cure her with their ayurvedic herbs. Rama Iyer, who was a daily visitor to the palace, begged the Maharani to allow him to treat her with a homemade remedy. The Rani agreed, and Rama Iyer went home and asked his wife to prepare a curry out of pickled mango seed. After removing the fleshy portions for pickling, the mango seeds would be preserved in salt and dried. This pickle was known as *adamangai*.

It was supposed to be a sovereign remedy for stomach disorders, especially the dysentery type. The curry was made with the *adamangai* and other ingredients, and Rama Iyer took it to the Rani and asked her to mix a little of it with rice and have it for three days with lunch. After three days, the Maharani was relieved of the griping pain, the loose motions stopped, and she was cured. The Maharaja and Maharani were pleased and wanted to reward Rama Iyer. The Maharaja asked Rama Iyer to ask for any favour and it would be granted.

The simple pious soul that great great grandfather was he could not think of anything. At last when it was pointed out to him that he should make a request, he hesitatingly asked for a sari for his wife—a *Chandravali* sari. This type of sari was just the fashion then and many rich ladies wore it. It was a silk sari, with horizontal lines in a contrasting colour running through the length. It cost four rupees only. A parcel containing the sari and a blouse piece was delivered to his house. The Maharaja, who was amused at the simplicity of the man, graciously on his own, granted a plot for him to build a house.

Rama Iyer had the land, but how was he to build a house without the wherewithal? The Crown Prince was a friend of his. Rama Iyer told him his problem. The Prince suggested that he should come to the back of the palace at night. A huge pile of timber was stocked in the courtyard. The Prince would throw a dozen logs of wood over the boundary wall and Rama Iyer could cart them home. In a week's time Rama Iyer had stocked enough timber to build his house. The roofing in those days consisted of wood rafters thatched with palm leaves. The supporting pillars were of thick wood. Rama Iyer's house was built, and it was handed down to his descendants. The house was later renovated and proper roofing and an upstair floor added to it. My father-in-law's stepbrother, who inherited it by virtue of his being a young boy when his father died, recently sold it for a handsome price of over a lakh rupees.

Pappu Anna, my great grandfather, was an interesting person. He was a gem merchant by profession. The story of how he came to take to this profession is worth recording. There was a Gujarati Seth, a wealthy jeweller living in Trivandrum, who was a friend of Pappu Anna. A fire broke out in the street where the Seth lived and his house was burnt down. In grief and anger the Seth left Trivandrum with his family and went to Bombay. Before leaving he told his friend Pappu Anna to take whatever he could salvage from the ruins. Pappu Anna set to work and took out a few broken pieces of furniture, which if mended could be used. As he was looking through the burnt house he discovered a badly burnt leather bag, containing within it a packet of precious stones, diamonds, rubies, emeralds, and other gems. I would like to believe that his happiness at his good fortune was tinged with sadness at the loss suffered by his friend, the Seth!

This was the nucleus of my great grandfather's business. Many anecdotes are told of his acumen in selling precious stones and gem-set jewellery. It seems he would visit affluent homes and when the ladies had assembled would pull out a case containing inferior quality stones set in gold and then hastily put it back in exclaiming, 'What a fool I am! This is too expensive, I will show you something good and cheaper.' This would arouse the ladies' curiosity and they would insist he show them the 'expensive' goods. They would end up buying inferior gems at a higher price. But they also say that he did not cheat them entirely and saw to it that they got a good bargain for the price. Anyway all is fair in love and business. Pappu Anna was also a musician and played the *mridangam*.

Apart from interesting stories that come from Taikad, it was the place where I saw, for the first time, instances of people being 'possessed'. Ambujam had gone to her in-laws in Shencottah. There was a *maadan*, a stone representing a village deity, in the backyard. One night while going out into the backyard she took fright and from that day on she was possessed. She had hysterical symptoms, bouts of weeping and laughing, and sometimes she would faint and lie unconscious for more than an hour. She would carry on for days without food. On some days, she would be normal, but suddenly she would become silent, and noticing her we would know she was getting possessed. My father-in-law called in a priest who was learned in such matters, and a lot of money was spent in an elaborate puja to drive off the spirit. Strange to say it did work. Afterwards she and her husband went to Rameswaram for further purification ceremonies.

In those days it was not uncommon for someone to become 'possessed' by a known or unknown spirit. Mama used to relate to us how during grandfather's time many of the family members became 'possessed' at one time or the other. Traditional society in Kerala is known for the practice of black magic. Any altercation could result in one of the parties (perhaps both) cursing the other family by invoking evil spirits on them. While some resorted to black magic themselves, the usual practice was to go to a professional *Tantrika*, a skilled black magic performer. The victims were usually women, and my own mother had been subjected to its cruel effects. Perhaps women were mentally and physically more vulnerable to 'possession'. My grandfather spent a lot of money engaging *Tantrikas* to counter the evil effects of black magic on the members of his family.

In South India there are specific temples where possessed women are brought to be cured by the deity. One such temple—the Chottanikarai Bhagavati temple—is near Trichur in Kerala. One could see swaying women, their hair open and eyes red. Some were violent. They were usually made to stay in the temple for forty-one days, and the priest would sprinkle consecrated water on them every day. Interestingly, the main offering to the deity in this temple is a medicinal ball made of dried ginger and herbs. The reigning deity is a powerful manifestation of the Goddess Parvati. She is endowed with the power to cure all ailments including madness and possession. Gunasekharam in Tiruchirapalli is another place where possessed women are brought for healing.

These experiences were chilling, but the most heart-rending experience that is still etched in my memory was that of being suddenly awakened at 3 in the morning and hearing my mother-in-law wailing lamentations. Sarojem had passed away.

Sarojem was married to one Hariharan, son of Trichur Ananthakrishna Iyer. He was a graduate and given a job by my father-in-law in the Devasthanam (Temple Trust) as a clerk.

Sarojem was fair and beautiful and had a sparkling intellect and a lively disposition. Hariharan perhaps treated her harshly and caused her a lot of unhappiness. That is the impression everyone had of him, but she was devoted to him and was proud of him. Once all of us had gone to Nagercoil for worship in the temple. Hariharan had instructed that *prasadam* from the temple be sent to us. This special *prasadam* consisted of a full seven-course meal with huge *papadams*, called *Valliya papadams*, and two *payasams*. Sarojem was so proud of her husband's authority. She had a cardiac problem, which today could have been treated and kept under control. But fifty-two years ago many of the medicines now available were not known. She was again in the family way, having had an abortion earlier, and in her eighth month of pregnancy her heart could not stand the strain and she passed away after an attack.

Dr Krishnan Pillai, our family doctor, had advised absolute rest. A nurse was appointed to look after her and take her pulse and give her medicines. It was on an afternoon, I think in February 1941, that she suddenly developed deep and laboured breathing. Her chest heaved up and down and she could not lie down. The nurse felt her pulse and in great agitation asked for the doctor to be called. Sarojem asked for some lime juice with a lot of sugar and when she drank it she said, 'Yes, it's very sweet and nice.' The next minute she asked for her husband, who had already been sent for, and with her eyes on the door she asked, 'Will I see him?' Then her breathing ceased suddenly, and our darling Sarojem left us forever, the smiling, sparkling, vivacious Sarojem who made fun of everything and everybody was gone. Hariharan was a minute too late. This was my first experience of seeing death so close. Sarojem, Ambujam and I were great friends and I just could not understand or accept that death could come so suddenly.

The ritual of death consisted of lamentations. These lamentations were sung in a mournful tune with words of endearment and praise for the departed loved one. At the end

of every line there would be a deep sob, called *Oppari* or
Pilakanam. There were women who specialized in wailing these
lamentations in a weird tune. At a formal mourning, these
women were engaged and paid to weep. The custom was and
continues to be vigorously practised among the non-Brahmins
and lower castes.

Sarojem's death hit Kunjaman Appa most. He called out her
name loudly from the front verandah a number of times and
after that he never uttered her name as long as he lived. Her
death broke his heart, and he was never the same man again.
He did not live long after that and died the way he lived, a
character out of the *Puranas*—many called him Bhishma. He
was conscious till the last breath and gave instructions about
who was to do his last rites. With full knowledge that each one
of us was giving him Ganges water, he put his hands across his
chest and passed away. A scion of the family had passed away!
In those days a death like Appa's was considered a fulfilled life.
The average life span was only fifty for men and fifty-five for
women, and Appa's having lived for seventy-seven years was
an event to be celebrated with feasting.

Sarojem's death was a tragedy, the grief very private. Only
my mother-in-law lamented, wailing the *Oppari*. The death of
wives was never mourned, though the death of the husband
was always mourned. This was perhaps because society
sanctioned and, in fact, expected the man to remarry. Only the
parents would mourn the death of their daughter. It took me
a long time to understand why my mother-in-law was the only
one wailing the *Oppari*. In the case of Kunjaman Appa, it was
a public mourning with all the relatives participating. Every
morning the priests came for chanting daily mantras and for
performing obsequies before a stone in which the spirit of the
dead person had been evoked by the mantras. Before this, the
women would gather in a circle on the front porch and singing
songs of lament would beat their breasts and go round and
round in a circle. There were old ladies proficient in the art of

Oppari, singing them in a weird, wailing tune. My mother-in-law used to get up at 3 a.m. and sing the *Oppari* for Appa as a matter of routine, something I found strange and somehow unpleasant. Perhaps by making grief so routine they took away its sting. Thus the ceremonies went on for thirteen days. Poor Lakshman, who was only thirteen at the time, had to perform all the rites. The little children watching these scenes picked up the wailing tune and the words and for some days to come they would be included in their play.

It is impossible to convey the plaintive tone in which *Oppari* was sung, but I do remember the words. Here are two *Oppari* songs. The first is sung by the daughter(s) on the passing away of the father:

> In the north, were paddy fields
> Also plantain groves
> Till my parents lived
> Pongal would bring me gifts from home
> With parents passing away
> I lost their plantain greetings
> I lost the pongal gifts
> In the south were paddy fields
> Also coconut groves
> Till my caring parents lived
> Annually I received the pongal gifts
> My caring parents passed away
> No more coconut greetings for me
> No more pongal gifts for me

Another song laments the loss of the father-in-law who had held the joint family together:

> Wise in bringing up (children)
> Able in all things
> Protecting and guiding the children

Correcting the grandchildren
Leaving the children in the street
Hastening to go before
Protecting and guiding the children
Wise enough to counsel the king
Leaving your children orphaned
Where did you disappear?

On the thirteenth day all the relatives and friends were invited to a grand feast. In the evening the family members, dressed in new clothes bought for that occasion went to the temple. Sweets and savouries were distributed to all the relatives and friends. This custom is still prevalent, even in urban areas as far away as Delhi and Mumbai, but the lamentations are no longer sung and there is no public display of grief.

The death of Sarojem reminds me of another practice connected with death, which is unique to South Indians. Sarojem had died when she was barely twenty. Since the woman had died while she had not yet delivered the child, the husband had to expiate the sin of making her carry a load she was not freed from. The expiation was undertaken by building a large cement seat where travellers could stop by and obtain temporary relief by setting down their baggage. This large stone is called a *chumai thangi*, literally, 'the bearer of burdens.' Hariharan built such a memorial for Sarojem. I am reminded of a *chumai thangi* built by one Mr V. Iyer in memory of his wife. My daughter Vijaya and I came across it in the course of our regular walks in Summer Hill. The *chumai thangi* is old and was probably built during the turn of the century. We wondered who the unfortunate Mr Iyer was and why he came to settle in Shimla, the summer capital of the British. We will never know the answer.

1942 came. It was over a year since Sarojem's death. The war, which began in 1939, had engulfed Asia. The Japanese had bombed Colombo. There was stray bombing in

Madras, and people from the city moved away to the countryside.

My father-in-law would go to a neighbour's house to listen to the news. Radios had just made their appearance and not every house owned one. He came home and reported the news to us. My mother-in-law was worried about her sons in Colombo. My father was in Kandy, and my husband and his younger brother Mani in Colombo. Letters and telegrams were sent, asking them to return. My father-in-law was feeling the strain of bearing the burden of the family and wanted his older sons back. After great pressure Mani came back. He was so angry and ashamed that he had to leave his brother behind and come back alone. Due to great pressure from the home front my husband also came back, resigning from his job in Reuters. If it were not for the fact that one did not defy one's parents, both of them would have preferred to stay back in Colombo right through the war years.

My eldest sister-in-law, Krishnambal, came with her family of eight children as evacuees from Madras. The house was full. How my mother-in-law managed to feed all of them is a wonder! Everyone was depressed about the future. My father-in-law was an irrepressible optimist. He never allowed his sons to feel depressed, but encouraged them and discussed plans with them. One day he brought home a Mangalore Brahmin priest, Annu Pothi. This man had retired as chief priest of the Nagercoil Temple, a temple to Nagaraj, the snake god. There was a big snake pit, which was the abode of many snakes. The priest performed puja at the pit, and offerings of milk and sweets were made. He then put his hand into the pit and took out some mud and that was distributed as *prasad*. The priest who performed this ritual had to live a pure and disciplined life. Any lapse on his part and the snakes would have bitten him when he put his hand inside the pit. Annu Pothi was a good astrologer and an interesting talker. He used to come to our house about eleven in the morning after his lunch and would sit till the evening.

The male members all finished their meals by 10 o'clock and were ready for him in the front porch. The porch of our house in Taikad was a large room with low walls on the sides. The front of the porch had some ten steps leading to the doorway. There were cement *pyols* on both sides where people could sit; chairs were also placed in the middle. The house was on a higher plane and was breezy; hence its name, *Pavana Vilas*, literally 'windy house.'

As soon as Annu Pothi came he would take centreseat and the horoscope book would be brought out. Women did not participate in these meetings. Sometimes Krishnambal Akka sat with them, but it was mainly the men who sat and chatted. Annu Pothi was consulted about the job prospects and future of the elder sons. His predictions were full of good forecasts and he would support his predictions by giving the favourable aspects of the planets as evidence. His predictions were a real morale booster and gave hope to our depressed hearts. My father-in-law had retired from service, but one or two peons out of loyalty still stayed on to help in the cooking. That was some relief for my mother-in-law, who was finding it hard to provide for such a large number of people. But for us youngsters it was fun to have the children.

I had my husband back with me and I was very happy. In those days we did not talk to each other when others were present, but our looks spoke an equally eloquent language. My husband would come to the ladies' quarter on some excuse or the other to talk to his mother or sisters, but more with the intent of getting a glimpse of me. When I first came to my in-laws' house I used to call my mother-in-law, *mami* (aunt), but my husband called me aside and told me I need not call her anything, neither *mami* nor *amma*, as that would be too familiar for a daughter-in-law. So as long as she lived, I never directly addressed her, but would talk to her without addressing her.

A well-known drama company, Rajamanikkam Co., came to Trivandrum and performed for a month in a theatre near our house. The dramas were mostly mythological plays. We had all made plans to attend a few plays, which started only at 10 p.m. Except for my mother-in-law, who never cared for any such entertainment, and the little children, the rest of us were to go after dinner. I was excited at the prospect. Besides I was also wondering if I would be allowed to sit next to my husband. I had been having a severe headache for two or three days and on the night of the show I was sick and feverish. I tried not to show my suffering lest I be asked to stay behind. That night I was too sick to even enjoy the drama and was almost on the point of asking my husband to take me home, but I gritted my teeth and held on. After we came home at 2.30 a.m., I developed a high fever. Next day our family doctor Dr Krishna Pillai was called, and he suspected typhoid. It was confirmed by the blood test and for a month I was in bed. There were no antibiotics in those days and typhoid had to run its course of three weeks. The only cure was a strict diet and bed rest. My temperature came to 99.8 deg. F. and remained there with an increase in the evening temperature for several days. I was given only liquids. I had become thin and weak; my hair was all matted, as no one would come near me to comb it. I must have been a fright to look at. All my waking and sleeping hours, I dreamt of food. My daughter Manju was kept away from me. That was the only major illness in my life; otherwise I have never been sick. During this time I had my monthly menses, another reason for keeping me isolated. When the doctor declared that I was all right and could be given a bath, there was a discussion over who could come near me and help me bathe. My husband said he would do it and he came to my room, put a little oil on my hair, and gently combed it. It was so matted that he had to cut some knots. My head was full of lice and as he combed, they all fell onto the towel he had put around me. It was so sweet of him to take such tender care of me. He kept the hot water ready, made me sit on a stool and bathed me, and then went to have his bath to remove the 'pollution' of touching me. After I had my bath, my sister-in-law brought a bucket of hot water and poured it over my head, and handed a towel to me, only then could I dry myself. All the clothes I had worn were soaked in a bucket and the maid took them to the river for washing. I felt so weak I could hardly stand. But gradually, I regained my health.

This kind of orthodoxy was new to me. My mother had also observed some of these rules and during our menses we were made to stay in a separate room, but it had an attached bathroom and was airy and sunny, with access to the garden. The three-day quarantine was so comfortable: we could read novels, listen to music and have such a good time that we looked forward to our monthly periods.

In my in-laws' house it was very different. In almost all houses in those days there was an inner quadrangle with an open space in the centre. The rooms, small dingy ones, were all on one side of the quadrangle. We had three rooms on the side, and the middle room, which had a door opening outside, was our menses room. I used to feel so scared of sleeping alone, so distant from the rest. I used to keep awake and start at every sound. Thevoo Akka's daughter Padma was about five years old and was a sick baby with a liver complaint. Her tummy was so big, she couldn't walk. She was also a petulant, troublesome child and would have tantrums. She would wake up quite often in the night and start howling. Thevoo Akka would have to mix Horlicks for her. All this would take an hour, and I would close my eyes and snatch the much-required sleep, blessing Padma.

On the fourth day of the menstruation I had to bundle my clothes and the utensils I had been using during the past three days and go to the tank to have a purifying bath. Only if one immersed oneself in water would the purification be complete. For a girl accustomed to bathrooms and showers, this was an ordeal.

I remember my husband narrating to me the story of how he had his first haircut, which was sometime in the early 1930s. He used to have an orthodox tuft, as became a good Brahmin, and also earrings called *kadukkan,* worn by boys and men. Ramaswamy had joined college and taken English Literature as his subject. Reading English novels and learning about modern society made him ashamed of keeping a tuft—it seemed like a backward thing to do. One fine morning he went to the barber and acquired a crop. He was, however, terrified of the reaction of his parents, aunts, and uncles, and the storm he would encounter at home. His father might have been a zealous reader of English fiction, but he would not appreciate the sacrifice of the tuft. His mother would, of course, be furious. So he sheepishly walked into the house through the back door, his cropped head hidden beneath a thin towel. His compassionate sisters fed him. His sisters could not shield him for long and word got out. Ramaswamy's removal of the tuft was the talk of the Pavana Vilas household for many days. Ramaswamy stayed away from his home for a fortnight till the storm blew over. Interestingly, his brother Mani's hair crop had a much smoother passage. There were some muted voices of protest and that was that.

In October 1942, my husband and I along with Manju went to Salem. My husband had decided to go to Delhi to try for a job. After a week in Salem we went to Tiruvannamalai to take the *darshan* and blessings of Sri Bhagavan Ramana Maharishi. Manju was just two and a half years old. Bhagavan would look at her with great kindness and love. He would beckon to her to come to him and pat her. My next visit to Tiruvannamalai was made when Manju was a little older and would dance prettily before Bhagavan, singing to herself. Ramana would look with happiness at her. From there my husband went by bus to Madras and then by the Grand Trunk Express to Delhi. I went back with my mother to Salem.

III

NEW DELHI

Eventful Years

❦❦❦

I came to Delhi in 1943. It was wartime. The year was a critical one and no one knew how long the war would go on. New Delhi was full of refugees from Burma. The news coming through, from the West and the East, was alarming.

Daddy and Mamma were in Trivandrum with Goma. My husband had sent me money for my ticket and was anxious for me to join him. I could not go to Madras alone without an escort. I requested Pamanji Anna to come with me, but Anna would not stir himself to leave Salem. Neither would his brother Thambi *mama*. Both had never done a spot of work in their lives. The house, the paddy fields, and the money their father had left for them was enough for them to lead a comfortable life. Pamanji Anna was a good homeopath and his treatment and medicines were free for patients.

After repeated requests from me, Anna bestirred himself sufficiently to go to his brother's house just down the road. He talked to his brother and gave glowing descriptions of the excellent snuff available at Madras, of which he could buy himself a generous stock if only he would escort me to Madras. The snuff (he used a superior variety called *thanga bhasmam*) decided the matter. Thambi *mama* came with me to Madras, bought his snuff financed by his brother and returned to Salem the next day.

In those days there was only one train—the Grand Trunk Express—connecting Madras and Delhi. I was travelling with Manju, who was three years old in a third class compartment with no doors. Coming from the sleepy little town of Salem where newspapers were seldom read, my first real brush with the war atmosphere was the presence of soldiers in the train that carried me to Delhi. My husband met Manju and me at the station, and we went home to Todarmal Lane.

British war propaganda agencies in the Capital were overcrowded with journalists, and writers were gainfully employed in New Delhi. One could see khaki all around. We, as ordinary citizens, used to gawk at white soldiers—American, British and Australian—moving about in their jeeps. There were innumerable Indian soldiers as well, but we took their presence for granted. Though the Americans appeared a little superior to the others, on the whole they all seemed to get along sportingly. The four theatres in Connaught Place, all showing only English films, were crowded in the evenings with this effusive crowd, together with foreign women and good-looking Anglo-Indian girls. The old city was out of bounds for them. Those were the days of emotion and excitement; the 'days of brave men and fair women.' This went on for many days, communications being tardy and future troop movements enveloped in a haze of uncertainty. We sometimes found the khaki hilarity in Delhi amidst so much war anxiety somewhat oppressive.

My husband was already in Delhi in search of a job. Interestingly, we had met the great sage Ramana Maharishi to secure his blessings for this momentous step. In my visits to the Ramana Ashram, what I remember most about Bhagavan are his luminous eyes and the closeness and warmth which birds and animals felt in his presence, reminiscent of what one has read about Saint Francis of Assisi.

My husband came to Delhi in 1942 and stayed in the Madras Hotel in Connaught Place for some time. My father recommended a job in the Government Press for my husband, but he refused to join as a clerk in any government office. He joined the All India Radio as a sub-editor on a salary of Rs 400. In those days AIR was in Old Delhi, fifteen miles from New Delhi.

He first stayed with his old friend 'Paramount' Krishna Iyer who was with him in Colombo, and then shifted to Madras Hotel, the refuge of all South Indians in Delhi. Mani joined him there. 'Paramount' Krishna Iyer was the distributor of Paramount Pictures to the local theatres and knew many of the theatre hall owners.

Recalling Krishna Iyer takes me back to the days when they had all been together in Colombo. Krishna Iyer had insisted on taking his friends Ramaswamy and Mani to a film on free passes. They were reluctant and were willing to pay, but Krishna Iyer wanted to 'show off' that he could take them to the balcony seats, the highest class, free. He asked them to wait till the lights went off and the show had started, since till then they could not enter the hall. When he told them in a whisper, 'Now get in,' they began to slink in the dark towards their seats. My husband and Mani were feeling like ticket-less viewers and they could not enjoy the film. They swore that they would never again go in for a free pass.

Memories of another film and the woes of an intrepid borrower come to my mind. The Chettiars as a community are rich merchants and businessmen; they are like the Banias of Gujarat. In Colombo they owned most of the big business houses. But, as in everything, there were exceptions, and there was one such exception among the Chettiars in Colombo. The Chettiars had a funny way of pronouncing and writing their initials. For example, Rama Krishna Muthu Rama Chettiar was pronounced Ravanna for R, Kavanna for K, Mavanna for M, Ravanna for Rama Chettiar. The Chettiar I mentioned earlier was Rama Linga Sundara Moorthy—Ravanna, Lavanna, Savanna, Mavanna Chettiar. He had tried his hand at several businesses, for which he had borrowed heavily and had incurred enormous losses.

Someone advised him to hire a theatre and show the most popular Tamil movie of those days, *Chintamani*. It was the story of the Saint Bilwamangal who was obsessed with a dancing girl, and had been told by her that if he only loved God as much as he loved her, he could attain salvation. There was sudden enlightenment and he became a saint. This film ran on the screen for two years in India. So the Chettiar hired a theatre for a month and bought the film. He expected to make his fortune in a month.

The first day the Chettiar was at the counter supervising the sale of tickets. There were among the crowd a few people known to the Chettiar—his creditors. They greeted him with gusto, so he graciously did not take money from them and sent them in, telling the doorman '*Vidu Vidu*' (*Vidu* in Tamil mean slet go). The next day more people to whom he owed money came with their friends and relatives, and as each day passed the number of '*Vidu Vidu*' swelled. The word had got around that Ra, La, Sa, Ma Chettiar was showing the film *Chintamani* in his theatre. The poor man tore his hair and, at the end of the month, found the collection did not even cover his expenses.

In Delhi, brother Mani had joined my husband and taken up a job. My brother Anantha joined them a little later. A classmate of my husband, one Mr Sampath, and his family were staying in a rented house in Todarmal Lane, near Barakhamba Road, New Delhi. He was transferred and gave the house to my husband. No. 10, Todarmal Lane was where I lived when I first came to Delhi with my three-year-old daughter Manju in 1943. The rent was Rs 25 and eight annas.

My husband's first job was as an AIR news sub-editor. He used to cycle all the fifteen miles to AIR, which was in Old Delhi beyond the present university area, for night duty. He would come back in the morning and his brother Mani would ride the cycle to his office. Between them they shared the cycle and the two carrier meals brought from the hotel, which was all they could afford. Before he got the AIR job, my husband was cooling his heels waiting for an opening. He was depressed staying in a street where all the male members went out to work. He would lock the front door and not open it till evening. He wrote his first short story there and sent it off to *The Hindu*, Madras. He was pleasantly surprised to find it in print the next week: *Gone With the Crowd*—by P. Ramaswamy. It brought him fifty rupees—much needed financial relief.

At this time he also had a strange experience. After seeing Bhagwan Ramana Maharishi in Tiruvannamalai before coming to Delhi, he was drawn to him and would pray to him. One night he had a dream that Bhagwan Ramana Maharishi was gently stroking his head and telling him not to worry and whispered a mantra in his ear. To the very last day of his life my husband never failed to repeat that mantra every morning in his prayers. It was soon after this that he joined AIR as sub-editor. However, he did not hold the job for long. Various factors contributed to his quitting. Firstly, he did not know shorthand, an essential qualification for a journalist. Secondly, he did not get on well with his boss, Mr Bonot, an Englishman who, my husband used to tell me, was generally nervous and irritable, though he did occasionally smile at nothing in particular. Mr Bonot, however, had the somewhat double-edged good fortune of being married to a beautiful wife.

It was the job of the sub-editor to monitor the BBC news and take it down in shorthand verbatim before writing up the daily news bulletins for AIR. Since he was trained at Reuters my husband could manage a good write up, but Mr Bonot insisted on shorthand. Everyday they had a press briefing with

Mr Bonot. Each one of them had to report on the highlights of the day, including national, provincial, and foreign affairs One day, someone said, 'Rajkumari Amrit Kaur has gone to New York. I don't know what she is doing there.' The chief replied in all seriousness, 'I see.' Mr P. Ramaswamy burst out laughing even though he tried to pinch himself to tears. The laughter was prompted by the dubious reputation of the Rajkumari, which found mention in the many veiled stories about her escapades in the Indian press. The next week he was out of a job without even a character certificate. Now there were three of them in 10, Todarmal Lane as by now Anantha had joined the Secretariat as an upper division clerk in the government.

My husband happened to meet Mr R. Subrahmaniam— 'Desini' to his friends—who was the Personal Assistant to Mr R. Natarajan, a big shot in the media. My husband must have shared with Desini his depression about being out of a job. It so happened that Mr Maqbool Mahmud, Secretary in the Chamber of Princes and a friend of Mr R. Natarajan, had asked him to recommend a good writer to write pamphlets for detailing the Maharajas' contribution to the war effort. These were aimed at glorifying the role of the Princes. Desini was sitting in the office when Mr Maqbool made his request. He at once thought of P. Ramaswamy and suggested to his boss that he knew a good writer who would fit the bill. Mr Natarajan asked Desini to request Ramaswamy to meet him. Desini came to Todarmal Lane. Finding the house locked, he slipped a note under the door asking Ramaswamy to meet Mr Natarajan. My husband got the job. When asked what salary he expected, in desperation he blurted out the figure of Rs 500. Mr Natarajan looked at him and wrote out a note to Mr Maqbool recommending a salary of Rs 500.

Mr Natarajan became a good friend of my husband. My husband never forgot Desini's timely help and was grateful to him. They remained good friends. After retirement, Desini settled in Bombay with his family and they kept up a steady correspondence. My nephew Chandran informs me that Desini died recently in Bombay. My husband would have felt very sad had he been here.

My understanding of politics broadened with my exposure to the politically charged atmosphere of Delhi. More importantly, my husband's profession led one willy-nilly to become involved in what was happening in the political scenario.

In 1943, there seemed to be a lull in the Indian national struggle. Politically, New Delhi was quiet. Lord Linlithgow was the Viceroy and after the Quit India declaration, he had ordered most Congressmen to be put behind bars. The political horizon was not merely quiet but bleak. I recollect the names of a few Congressmen—'not dangerous' I suppose from the British point of view because they were not under arrest—taking up service under the princes and some even becoming *Dewans* of small states. Later (after Independence), some of them rose to become Ministers in our Government. Secretaries became Ambassadors, an outstanding example being Mr K.N. Panikar, who was free India's Ambassador in China and elsewhere. The Communists had gone underground during the first phase of the war, and it was only when Russia joined the Allies that the Indian Communists began supporting the war effort, calling it now the People's War.

Sixty years hence, 1943 seems to have receded into history. Yet, New Delhi in 1943 seemed suspended in time with the end of the war nowhere in sight. There was a lot of furore about the war in the press and the radio. We felt the tension and yet curiously we were not a part of it. Life followed a dull, dragging routine. The soldiers and the refugees were the sort of intruders who, we hoped, were in transit and would soon pass. For the women, war conditions imposed a rationing of rice and wheat. Cloth was not freely available, and we had to buy our daily wear cotton saris from authorized ration shops and were allowed only a limited quota. Kerosene and coal were rationed. The rice supply was so meagre that we used to make rice for the men and wait eagerly to see if they would leave any rice for us. We almost pounced on the leftover rice because as South Indians we were not roti-eaters, but were now compelled to make wheat our staple diet. I felt that we were suffering the brunt of a war that had nothing to do with us. It was ironical that on the one hand we were fighting for our independence from the British and on the other we were fighting for the British in a war which was not ours.

My husband and I lived in 10, Todarmal Lane for two happy years. We were in Todarmal Lane during the end of war. There were American and British soldiers stationed in Delhi. But, one could go out and return late in the night; there was no fear of robbers or murderers. Mani had taken up another job and gone to Bombay and my brother and his wife Saroja had shifted to a rented house. In 1946, they had their only son Ramanan who was born to them by the blessing of Bhagavan Ramana after many years of marriage. Ramanan was to become the constant playmate and companion of my children.

A friend of ours, Ramakrishnan, who belonged to sister-in-law Thevoo's village at Krishnapuram in Tirunelveli district, was staying with us along with his wife Rajamma. They had no children. He had his office, the India Publicity Office, in our front room, which used to be our drawing room. They occupied the front bedroom and we the back room. Such friendships are rare these days. We lived like one family. Ramakrishnan's staff consisted of a lone typist Mr Janakiraman, also from his village. Ramakrishnan was strict about his office timings. He would enter his office at 10 a.m. through the front verandah, unlocking the office door and would come out only at 2.30 for a coffee break. Then at 5.30 p.m. he would lock the door and was back home from office.

My husband would leave early for his office, the Chamber of Princes. Event since he began writing the war pamphlets,

Maqbool had absorbed him in the regular staff as an Under Secretary. Maqbool was a hard taskmaster and Ramaswamy a willing worker, and he worked himself to the bone. He would come home late at night, sometimes at eleven or twelve. At times he would sleep in the office, if it became very late. Many, many days he would not have lunch and dinner in the house. Ramakrishnan used to feel sorry for him, especially when Rajamma cooked his favourite dishes. One day he decided he would not eat till Ramaswamy had lunch. He wore a dhoti, tied a cloth on his head to keep off the heat, took the food in a tiffin carrier, and went by bus to the Chamber of Prince's office, which was in a wing of what is now Parliament House. Ramaswamy was shocked to see his friend bringing his lunch like a peon and was very moved. After that he tried very hard to at least have lunch before leaving for office.

Ramakrishnan, Rajamma and both of us with Manju used to go for night shows to the theatres at Connaught Place. The show started at 9.30 p.m. and was over around midnight. We used to come back walking, as Barakhamba Road is very near Connaught Place. Tickets were available before the show began, and unlike today there was no need to book them in advance. As it was wartime, the hall was full mainly of soldiers and their wives or lady companions. Before the film started there would be a few minutes of community singing, an entertainment for the soldiers. Old popular songs would be flashed on the screen and the voices of great singers of those days like Sir Harry Lauder would sing the songs with a message flashed on the screen for the audience to join in the chorus. I remember the song *It's a long long way to Tipperary* coming on the screen. In the chorus, the men in the audience would imitate a female treble and sing the ladies' parts! We would walk back home and Ramakrishnan, who was full of humour and a good mimic, would regale us with witty anecdotes. Manju would usually have gone to sleep, and the men would take turns carrying her.

My childhood indifference and carelessness still continued. One day I removed my gold chain and did not remember where I had kept it. I was scared of being scolded by my husband and was in tears. When Ramakrishnan came home from his front room office, Rajamma broke the news to him. He became serious and when my husband got back—he had come home early that day—they both were very concerned and were thinking of informing the police. I don't know what she saw in their faces that made Rajamma suspicious. She suddenly turned to me and said, 'Sethu, there is nothing to worry; these two have taken the chain and kept it. I know it, I can see it in their playacting.' I was not so sure, but was hoping that what Rajamma had said was true. Both denied this vehemently, but Rajamma stood her ground and went about her work with a carefree air. At last Ramakrishnan sheepishly told his friend, 'This wife of mine is too shrewd, I say, we cannot hide the truth anymore.' And the chain was brought out and handed over to me with a warning not to let this happen again.

How both the men used to make fun of us! Rajamma and I were learning to knit sweaters. After knitting a good length, we would make a mistake and not having learnt the art of rectifying it, we would unravel the knitted fabric. Having proudly shown our husbands our progress, the next day would find one of us with an unravelled ball of wool. Our individual progress was more or less the same, but the unravelling part was a sure thing. They would tease us and Ramakrishnan would say: 'Ramaswamy, we would do well to go and buy ourselves sweaters from the shop. By the time they knit ours, we will be old.' Nevertheless, we did complete two good sweaters for our husbands.

Manju was then three years old and was a sweet playful child. When my husband returned from the office, she would run and hide herself. He would have to make a pretence of searching for her and scolding her for going outside to the railway line. She could not bear to wait in hiding even for a few minutes, but would come out from her hiding place and say, 'Appa, I fooled you.' In my family, my brother and two elder sisters called my father Papa. My two younger sisters and I called him Daddy. My children called their father Appa and me Amma in the traditional South Indian way.

Manju had this habit of running outside to the railway line, which was only a few yards away at the end of the street. In those days the G.T., the only train from Madras, passed through Todarmal Lane. Even today the trains from Madras, the Grand Trunk Express and the Tamil Nadu Express pass through Todarmal Lane and our house (No. 10) can be seen from the train. Manju would stand, hands on hip, and watch the trains pass by. We were scared lest she stepped onto the track and not notice a train coming. Ramakrishnan cured her of this habit by making her stand on a chair, then shouting at her and using loud threats. He never beat her, but because of his loud scolding she became afraid of him and stopped going near the railway track.

At this time, a friend of ours Mr P.D. Murthy was transferred from Lahore. He was DPIO (Deputy Principal Information Officer) in the Information and Broadcasting Ministry. My husband used to stay with him whenever he went to Lahore on official business. Murthy, his wife and two children stayed with us for a month till they moved to their Government quarters. His eldest son Prakash was a little older than my daughter Manju, and the daughter Lakshmi was a little younger. Mrs Murthy was a capable lady. They were Telugus. Prakash's name was later changed to Ashok, as Murthy did not find his son bright enough to justify the name (*Prakash* means light).

Before the Murthys came, Ramakrishnan and Rajamma left for Calcutta. Ramakrishnan's main office was in Calcutta, and he had to take charge there. He had appointed my sister-in-law Ambujam's husband, Lakshminarayan, to take his place here.

As I said earlier, in those days there was only one train running between Madras and Delhi, the Grand Trunk Express. The third class compartments would always be crowded since few people could afford first-class travel. People got in and got out through the windows. My husband went to the station to receive his brother-in-law. It was also the first time he had ventured out of his village Shencottah. As usual, he also had to be helped through the window with his luggage and he came home thoroughly exhausted. Lakshminarayan slept in the front verandah while the Murthys occupied the front room. The poor man must have been extremely tired and was talking, howling and making weird noises in his sleep. Murthy was a coward. I have never come across a grown man being so cowardly. Even to go to the bathroom at the back of the house, he would wake up his wife. He was frightened by Lakshminarayan's nightmares and couldn't sleep. Next day, he was extra nice to Lakshminarayan and in the evening took him to Connaught Place and gave him a treat. He wanted to put him in a happy mood so that he would sleep peacefully at night and not have nightmares. Whether it was due to Murthy's therapy or the fact that Lakshminarayan had recovered from the exhaustion, he slept well.

The Murthys left for their official quarters. Lakshminarayan, after two months of managing the office, was called to the Calcutta office and the Delhi office was closed.

During my first month in Delhi, I found cooking difficult. In those days charcoal and soft coke was used in tin or mud *angithis* (stoves). Charcoal was priced higher than soft coke. The method was to use a layer of charcoal and light the *angithi* and after the charcoal started burning, soft coke would be heaped on it. The heat was quite fierce and a meal could be cooked as quickly as it is now on a gas stove. But I did not know that soft coke could be used. I ordered one *maund* of charcoal and since charcoal is light I had to keep on replenishing the fire with more coal and the cooking took a long time. In time I learnt to use soft coke, to make rotis as well as a few North Indian dishes. We had a Garhwali boy working for us for Rs 20 a month.

I was still inexperienced in housekeeping. The shop from which we got our provisions—Shimla Stores in Panchkuian Road—would present inflated bills, underweigh items and duplicate orders. In those days when everything was so cheap, my provisions bill for just two adults and a child came to Rs 400 to Rs 500 a month, an astronomical figure. It was when the Murthys were staying with us that Mrs Murthy checked the bills and found irregularities in the billing. My deplorable housekeeping often provoked my husband to call me his 'Dora', the adorable but, inefficient child-wife of Dickens from *David Copperfield.*

Delhi, as I remember those days, was very different from what the city is now. The Delhi Transport Corporation was not in existence, nor were there taxis, auto rickshaws or the smokin' Harley Davidsons, popularly known as *phatphatis*, carrying ten people at a time. The only mode of transport for the public was the *tonga*. There was a tram service in some parts of the Old City. Today, the Delhi Metro Rail project proposes to use some of these earlier routes. In course of time, the *phatphatis* replaced the tongas and became the cheapest mode for travelling long distances within Delhi. Sometime in 1998, these vehicles were banned from the roads of Delhi, bringing to an end the era of the smokin' Harley Davidsons, which had served Delhi for many decades. Considering the quantum leap in vehicular traffic in Delhi, future travel in the Capital, in all likelihood, will be underground.

My husband was a member of a lending library paying a subscription of Rs 3 a month for two books at a time—there was no 'deposit' in those days. There were no pavement book shops; these appeared only when the British began leaving. They dumped all their books on second-hand book dealers and many people got some of their most precious possessions from them.

Among the popular writers of crime fiction were Edgar Wallace, Philips Oppenheim, Agatha Christie, and Peter Cheyney. Agatha Christie continues to be my choice of reading, although few people seem to read her these days. My favourite women writers were Mrs Henry Wood, Mary Corellie, Baroness Orzy, Margaret Kennedy and above all, Pearl S. Buck, who was to become the inspiration for the turning point of my life. Of these the present generation may have heard only of the last name.

Life was leisurely and living was easy. There was no rat race leading to unnecessary stress. It would make an interesting exercise to compare the prices of commodities in those days and the present. Milk was selling at 12 *seers* for a rupee and today it is 12 rupees or more a litre! One could buy vegetables for one rupee and manage to cook lunch and dinner, and still be left with stocks for the next day. Today even a beggar accepts a rupee with reluctance; *annas* and *paisas* count for nothing.

It was wartime, and there was rationing. The quota of rice was inadequate for rice-eaters like us. Mill cloth was available only in certain authorised shops. I have stood in the queue to buy a cotton sari from the Delhi Cloth Mills retail shop. The country was subjected to a lot of restraints, but still there was contentment. There was pleasure in reading books, writing, talking, and learning. There was no TV or multi-channeled cable to gag these interests.

In 1945, we shifted from Todarmal Lane to a first-floor flat in Daryaganj. The landlord, a radiologist, wanted his house back for private practice, so we moved to Daryaganj in old Delhi. We got this house through a friend. My brother and his wife Saroja stayed with us in Daryaganj.

I went to Coimbatore for my second delivery where Daddy, after leaving Ceylon during the war, was posted as Inspector of Civil Supplies. Lalita was born on 31 July 1945. She was a very pretty baby with large eyes and perfectly formed arched and pencilled eyebrows. Manju, my first daughter, was then five years old, a graceful and attractive child. She was imaginative and would make up stories. The doctor who attended on me was our family doctor and lived close to our house. He had no children. We had the cradle ceremony for the baby on the eleventh day and had invited some friends. A few days later Manju came in excitedly and told my mother, 'Anandamma (everyone called my mother by her name), doctor Aunty has got a baby, so many people are going to their house. Let us also go and see the baby.' Mama did not believe her and told her not to talk nonsense, but Manju was insistent. Mama went with her to the doctor's house. Of course, nothing like that had happened. Everyone had a good laugh. The child in her imagination had connected the cradle ceremony to a similar function in the doctor's house when she saw some visitors going to their house. She would stand in the front porch and point out to children passing by and say, 'They are my friends, one is Surya and the other Chandra.' I used to scold her for lying, but found that it was only her imagination at work. Later on when I read Saki's short story *The Open Window*, the little girl in the story reminded me of Manju.

I went back to Daryaganj when Lalita was only two months old. She caught a chill in the winter and developed a severe chest infection. Dr H.R. Dawar was a general practitioner with a clinic in Daryaganj. The first time we went to him was for Lalita, Lalloo, as we called her. Till his death in 1980 he remained our family doctor and friend. In course of time he prospered and moved to Sundar Nagar, a posh area in South Delhi, to his huge house. For my husband he was both physician and friend. Some time After Dr Dawar's death, my husband, who must have been around 77 at that time, was feeling unwell. Out of sheer force of habit he dialled Dr Dawar's number although he now had a different, much younger doctor. Mrs Dawar immediately recognized his voice and told him sadly, 'Mr Ramaswamy, your friend is no more. You have to call up a different doctor now.' I still remember the look of dismay on my husband's face.

In our Daryaganj home, we had a room at the top, on the terrace, and one Mr T.N. Saraf, a Kashmiri, stayed there with us for some time. He was a clerk under my husband in the Chamber of Princes. He used to go to Connaught Place and book tickets for us and for himself and that was the only service he did for us. The room was free. Almost every week we went to see an English movie. Mr T. R.V. Chari, my husband's boss in Reuters, Colombo, was posted somewhere in India. His younger brother, Varadarajan, Joo for short, was studying for his M.Com. in Delhi University, and Chari had asked us to put him up with us. Chari later left Reuters and joined the Information Ministry as Principal Information Officer in Delhi. So our small household in Delhi had an extended wing.

My husband was still in the Chamber of Princes. His boss Maqbool Mahmud became fond of him. When Mir Sahib came to know that we needed a cook, he appointed an orderly for our domestic work. Narayan Singh, a Garhwali, was a born cook. He knew the cuisines of Kashmir and the Punjab and could make South Indian dishes like *sambhar* and *rasam* as well. He was a middle-aged man and a real asset.

My husband had many Kashmiri friends through Saraf, among them R.N. Kaul and Bamzai, correspondent of the *Blitz*, the Bombay weekly whose editor was R.K. Karanjia. They would often meet at the India Coffee House in Connaught Place; sometimes for lunches and dinners in each other's houses. We lent the services of our Jeeves, Narayan Singh, on such occasions. They also used to meet in a Kashmir fur shop in Queensway, now Janpath. All Kashmiri items—shawls, fur, papier-mâché boxes and craft work were sold there. One of his friends was Mr Bakshi Gulam Mohammed who traded in salt, which was a precious commodity in Kashmir in those days and took it by truck to Kashmir. He later became Chief Minister of Kashmir and acquired the reputation of being the prime mover behind the eviction of the Kashmiri pundits from the Valley.

After the Chamber of Princes closed, T.N. Saraf went to

Mayurbunj State and took up a job as Private Secretary to the Maharaja there. Saraf was a versatile man; he was an engaging talker, played cards, drank in company and very soon became a favourite with the Maharaja. In those days there was a quota of nominations to the IAS. Saraf was recommended by the Maharaja and was nominated to the IAS. His rise was meteoric. He joined the UN on an assignment and made his fortune. He had four sons, and he could place them all in good jobs. He retired on a UN pension, settled down in Delhi, and built a posh house in Greater Kailash. In later years, we tried renewing our friendship, but found that Saraf was embarrassed whenever he saw us, so we lost touch with him.

Raghunath Kaul resigned from the police and joined Air India as Chief Traffic Manager. He had the opportunity to travel abroad and stay in important cities of the world. He had no children by his second wife. My husband told me Kaul had children by his first wife. We kept in touch and remained close friends.

It was 1946 and my husband was working wholeheartedly for the Chamber of Princes. A rather unusual story about the integration of the princely territories into the Indian union occurred at that time. These were politically crucial years since Sardar Patel was carrying out negotiations to reorganize the princely states. The Nawab of Bhopal was Chancellor and with his trusted lieutenant Mir Sahib was trying to mobilize the Muslim states together, backing Jinnah.

It was quite by chance that my husband met a friend, a junior Indian officer in the political department, and while talking, the friend exclaimed, 'What is your Nawab of Bhopal doing? He has sent a top secret letter to the Secretary of State for India and Lord Wavell (then Crown Representative) that the Princes would revolt if Britain came to a separate settlement with India.' My husband immediately knew it was 'hot' news and grasped the significance of this letter and its implications for the Congress. This letter was sent sometime in December

when Mr Nehru was about to go to London for the final phase
of negotiation with the Atlee Government. Very agitated, my
husband decided to act. Every Indian in those days was at heart
with the Congress and that was the impulse that had made my
husband's friend blurt out information. My husband felt that
he owed it to his country to disclose this important piece of
news to the press. After all, the information did not come from
his office, but from outside and he would not be committing
any breach of faith. Of course, his friend would have to be
protected. That evening at their meeting at India Coffee House,
the haunt of journalists then and now, my husband mentioned
the secret letter to Mr K.N. Bamzai, his friend. Bamzai's eyes
popped out since he knew my husband held a strategic job as
Under Secretary in the Chamber and he sat up. My husband
should have been more guarded about handing over such
information to the *Blitz*, which had the reputation of being a
sensational newspaper. Bamzai, after getting the news, promised
to abide by the conditions imposed on him by my husband. One
of the conditions was that he should get full confirmation from
the *Blitz* correspondent in London that such a communication
had actually been received. The other one, of course, was that
he should not reveal the source. He readily agreed.

The *Blitz* came out with a splashy front-page story about
the Nawab of Bhopal's letter. It quoted an 'unimpeachable
source' and had printed word for word what Ramaswamy had
told him. My husband, who was first and foremost a journalist,
was experiencing the bite from the other side of the Press.
However, Mr Bamzai was a close friend and the other Kashmiri
friends rallied round and assured him that 'nothing would
happen'. The Nawab denied writing the letter with the safety
clause, 'I did not write any such letter in my capacity as
Chancellor.' Ramaswamy happened to see this note in a file. I
don't think the editor waited to get confirmation from London.
The news created enormous ferment. It was news for many of
the Princes also. About a week later Bamzai and two other

Kashmiri friends came to our house and said that Mr Nehru wanted to meet Mr Ramaswamy. Jawaharlal Nehru was a hero in the eyes of every Indian, and for my husband, Nehru was his ideal from his school days. It was an honour to be sent for by him, but the purpose for which Nehru wanted to meet him, i.e., to ascertain the truth about the story, was not acceptable. My husband declined to be a squealer and politely refused to meet Nehru. Again he was pressurized by his friends to meet Nehru anywhere, at any place of his choice. My husband perhaps suspected that it was his friends and not Nehru himself who wanted to meet him. In any case he declined and that was the end of the matter. Fortunately, the plan of the Nawab did not work.

A few years later my husband was cycling to the GPO to send off a press telegram when Bamzai, who was driving a car, saw him and stopped. He was sorry to see his friend riding a bicycle, and remarked, 'If only you had listened to us and met Nehru, you would also be driving a car.' My husband thanked him and said he was happy as he was, with a clear conscience. I am able to recount this and other political stories, as my husband used to discuss office matters and confide in me. I also found some hand-written notes of his on this incident.

In 1946 we were in Daryaganj, and I was expecting my third child at the end of November. We had booked my confinement in Dr Sita Sen's Nursing Home in Daryaganj, an expensive place. In November, riots broke out. My mother had come to assist me. Suddenly one night we heard loud shouts of '*Allah Ho Akbar.*' All of us kept awake that night. The very next day, newspapers reported communal riots in the Walled City. Curfew was clamped. What followed were nights of terror. Sleep was fitful with screams reverberating in the night air. Our hardy Punjabi neighbours downstairs told us to keep boiling oil ready, to pour on the Muslim rioters if they came near our house. We were prepared with hot oil, hot water, and knives and sticks. The next morning our Muslim milkman warned us that we should leave Daryaganj, as there was danger to our lives.

Our family doctor Dr H.R. Dawar advised us to move to New Delhi, as my time was near and going to the nursing home during a curfew would be a problem. T.R.V. Chari, my husband's boss in Reuters, was in Delhi staying in Sujan Singh Park. We went to his house with a few things. Mr and Mrs Chari were good friends of ours. But when they saw my condition they were embarrassed and we could see they were reluctant to put us up even for a few days. God was kind to us and succour came in the form of a Trivandrum friend, a bachelor who had been allotted quarters in Lodi Colony. He said that we could stay there for a month or two. My husband assured him that he would be sending the baby and me by plane to Madras forty days after the delivery.

My third daughter Jayashree was born on 2 December 1946. We called her Jayashree, which means 'victory', because she had survived the Partition riots. Before the month was over we heard that Mr M.S. Ramayyar, Deputy Accountant General, was willing to let out a portion of his Lodi Estate bungalow. Those days the Government shifted to Shimla, its summer capital, so Ramayyar wanted a tenant who would take care of the house during the summer. He wanted us to vacate the house in September as he was expecting a transfer. We moved to 77, Lodi Estate. A few months later M.S. Ramayyar told us that his transfer orders were cancelled. The government had decided not to shift to Shimla for the summer and New Delhi would be the permanent capital. He asked us to stay on. The Lodi Estate bungalows were spacious houses with a left and right wing each and the drawing and dining rooms in the centre. There was a spacious lawn and gardens, with five servants' quarters at the back. We occupied the left wing. We had a large room, an office room in the front, a pantry which was converted into a kitchen, and a toilet-cum-bathroom. The old system of night soil being removed in buckets by *jamadars* was prevalent. Cooking gas had not come into domestic use; charcoal and soft coke were used.

In 1946 it had become obvious to everyone that Partition was inevitable. Britain had agreed to grant independence, but after amputating a portion of Bharat and creating a Muslim State, Pakistan, which Mr Jinnah would head. Mahatma Gandhi's earlier protests of 'Partition over my dead body' were not heeded. Nehru was in a great hurry to head the government of independent India. Mountbatten had hurriedly drawn up a plan demarcating the territories to be handed to Pakistan. It was at this time that the Princely State of Travancore shot into the news with its demand for autonomy and recognition as a separate state. The *Dewan* of Travancore, Sir C.P. Ramaswamy Iyer, was a wily Brahmin. His advice to the then Maharaja Chitra Tirunal was not to give in to coercion by Sardar Vallabhai Patel to accede to the Indian union. He egged on the Maharaja to press for an autonomous status. Sir C. P. had a national anthem for Kerala—*Vanchi Bhoomi.* After a show, Kerala theatres, would flash the Maharaja's picture on the screen followed by that of C.P. Ramaswamy Iyer with a recording of their particular national anthem. Everyone had to stand up in respect to the anthem. But in the royal family itself there was a fraction, which opposed the plans of Sir Iyer. Trivandrum, the capital of Travancore, suddenly became a hotbed of political intrigue.

In this context, there was an assassination attempt on Sir C.P. Ramaswamy Iyer. Its narrative comes to me from authentic family sources since our family had always maintained close links with the palace. The attempt occurred during a music concert by Sri Semmangudi Sreenivasa Iyer on the occasion of some state celebration. The concert was attended by His Highness the Maharaja as well as Sir Iyer. In the middle of the concert, the lights went off and Sir Iyer was attacked by an assailant with a knife. The assassin aimed at his throat. The people present said Sir Iyer was saved by the heavy silk folds of his *angavastram*, which he usually wound around his neck like a scarf. Sir Iyer escaped with just a slash on his cheek. One Sundaram Iyer, a school Head Master, jumped on the assailant and held on to him fearlessly till the assailant could be apprehended. The case was hushed up though rumours were rife about the political conspiracy behind the assassination attempt. Mr K. R. Kumaraswamy, a well-known musician and a contemporary of Chemmangudi (Mr Kumaraswamy is now 87), was present when this happened. He tells me that the assassination was the result of internal divisions within the royal family over the accession issue.

Meanwhile, the Chamber of Princes was on its last legs. Sardar Patel had done a tremendous job of reorganizing the states. Many of the Maharajas had acceded to India. The Nawab of Bhopal and his fellow men in other Muslim States had to eat humble pie and accede to India. The Chamber of Princes became redundant. It was a quirk of fate that my husband had to hand over the letter from the then Chancellor, the Nawab of Patiala, to his boss Maqbool Mahmud, relieving him of charge as Secretary of the Chamber on charges of insubordination. My husband had no choice, but to carry out the orders of the Chancellor, though it gave him a lot of pain to be the one to do it.

My husband never saw Maqbool again. But, a stenographer who had kept in touch with Mir Sahib told him that a few days before he died Mr Maqbool had written saying he was not angry with Ramaswamy and eagerly wanted to come to Delhi to see him again. Mir Maqbool died a tragic death in an air crash. A detail, which my husband told me about this remarkable man, still lingers in my mind. When Mir Maqbool knew the plane was going to crash he wrote out his last will and testament and packaging it ingeniously threw it out of the plane. This document was recovered and his will carried out!

On 15 August 1947 India became independent and the Chamber of Princes ceased to exist. My husband came home in the evening with a brick of ice cream. This was his way of telling me that he had lost his job at the Chamber. India had attained Independence, and he was now free to pursue a journalistic career. Our cook Narayan Singh had to leave our service. My husband found him a job in a government office in Bombay.

My husband came back to journalism after five years. It was an uphill task, as he did not join any newspaper on a regular basis. His first assignment was a weekly column in Nehru's own paper the *National Herald*, Lucknow, with the title *A Delhi Causerie* under the pen name Pertinax (adopted from a famous French columnist). He also worked for the *Pioneer*, Lucknow, and Mr K. Shiva Rao asked him to send articles to the *Manchester Guardian*, London.

There was no regular income, except for the payment from the *National Herald*. Even though I was not a good housekeeper, I was thrifty by nature and so we managed. My husband used to cycle to the GPO to send off his dispatches. After Jayashree was born, my mother took my second daughter Lalloo (Lalita) with her to Salem. Manju, by then, was going to school.

At about this time, the Associated Newspapers of Ceylon, which was a leading newspaper group publishing the *Ceylon Observer*, and the *Ceylon Daily News*, with Sinhalese and Tamil editions, and a dozen journals from Colombo wanted a correspondent in Delhi. After a trial period, my husband was hired on a permanent basis as correspondent. This was a turning point in our lives. He was paid a monthly salary of Rs 4000, very good payment in those days. Apart from news reporting, he was also writing a weekly column called *A Window on India*, which became extremely popular to the extent of bringing him fan mail! He now gave up his weekly column for the *National Herald*.

We were in Delhi in Lodi Estate during the 1947 riots. Mr M. S. Ramayyar and my husband were given civic duties and had to take turns keeping watch at night. There was nothing much in our area except Hindus looting Muslim shops. Old Delhi was worst affected. My husband was once travelling in a *tonga* driven by a Muslim to Connaught Place, when they were warned of the outbreak of violence. My husband got down and the poor *tonga* driver fled away. I am sorry to write that many educated 'Hindu' gentlemen brought home property looted from Muslim shops. Mr Ramayyar used to bring home valuable items, left behind by unfortunate Muslim families, and being sold for a song by Hindus. My husband and I were shocked at the callousness of those who capitalized on others' miseries.

We could now afford a car. Buying a car in those days was like buying a brick of ice cream. I mean it was as simple as that. We walked into Allenburys in Connaught Place, chose a Morris Minor, bluish grey in colour, paid the cheque, and got into the car. A driver from the firm drove us down to our house and that was that. My husband already knew how to drive. He had learnt it surreptitiously, using his father's car in Trivandrum during his college days. Within a week he was driving his car.

Jayashree was just a year old when I had my next baby. My fourth daughter Tara was born in Salem on 15 January 1948.

January 30: Mahatma Gandhi was assassinated. I was in Salem. My husband was in Delhi, but not at the fateful prayer meeting in Birla House where the shooting took place. His colleague and friend Mr Sailen Chatterjee, a staunch Gandhian, was there and was in shock for a week. We did, of course, attend Gandhi's prayer meetings often. The first time I saw Gandhiji was at a prayer meeting at the Ram Lila grounds. Looking at Bapuji, I was struck by his golden complexion. I thought then that he looked like a statue made of gold. It was much later that I came to know of the belief that people who led a very spiritual life developed a golden complexion. I remember his soft, indistinct speech which still had the power to move millions of Indians to adopt the path of passive resistance against the British. Ordinary people would walk for miles to go and listen to the Mahatma and join him in his favourite prayers including '*Raghupati Raghava Rajaram, patita pavana Sitaram.*'

The assassination of Mahatma Gandhi shook the entire country. It was a personal tragedy for every Indian. The first thought that sprang to everyone's mind was, 'The assassin must have been a Muslim.' Anticipating the likelihood of the anger of the people turning into acts of violence against Muslims, Prime Minister Jawaharlal Nehru as well as other Ministers went on air, repeatedly appealing to the people to be calm and announcing that the assassination was done by a Hindu, Nathuram Godse. This was what prevented a communal holocaust. We listened to the news fearfully, anticipating more riots, but violence was sporadic and soon brought under control.

I came back to Delhi with Tara, leaving Manju, Lalloo, and Jayashree with my parents. For me those were primarily years of child bearing and child rearing. I was pregnant nearly every year, and I wonder what I would have done with my small kids without the immense support provided by my parents. After my delivery I would come back to Delhi with my newborn, leaving the toddler and her sisters with my parents in Salem. Obviously, in those days pregnancies were not planned nor always desired. I ate great quantities of pineapple, papaya, hot chutney, and ginger in an effort to drop the baby but nothing worked. In my desperation I even tried long walks, jumping, and skipping, which we were told, were sure ways to abort, but it didn't work. I was subsequently grateful to God that despite my foolishness in resorting to such hazardous exercises, dangerous for both the mother and her foetus, my six girls were born absolutely healthy. I did have a couple of abortions, when my hazardous tactics worked.

Frequent pregnancies were a tribulation I shared with most women of my generation. Family planning was practically unknown and women conceived without a choice. Casualty rates were high, both among pregnant women and newborns. I remember that a woman who had successfully delivered would be greeted by women visitors with the phrase, 'cheththu pizhaichchiya', meaning 'Have you returned from the brink of death?'

A journalist's life has its thrills and excitement. But I soon found that being a journalist's wife was not easy. I had to be on my toes all the time, not knowing when my husband would go out and when he would come back. Night trips to the airport when foreign dignitaries came, press conferences, attending Parliament—all these kept him busy. He would suddenly drop in with friends, and I would have to provide meals or coffee and snacks, depending on the time of the day. At the end of the day he would be writing dispatches or typing them straight on to the typewriter, and rushing out to send them off by post or telegraphing it to Ceylon to meet his deadline. The fatiguing work of correcting the copies while he got ready and filing them away was left to me.

As my children grew up, I was burdened with more work. If the children did not get up early in the morning to get ready for school, I was to blame. Despite the chores of bathing the children, combing and plaiting the hair of six girls, just not having lunch laid out on the table would create a storm. If his pen or comb were misplaced, I would be blamed, leading to another storm. The stormy quarrels were frequent, but the storm was always from his side and the weathering from mine. Sometimes I felt so helpless that I would only weep or mutter to myself in the space I considered mine—the kitchen. This is not to say that my husband did not love me, but I couldn't understand his habit of blaming me for everything that went wrong.

We were getting almost all the local newspapers. The Ceylon Observer and Daily News would come by post. By the end of the month the newspaper pile would be enormous. But,

I was not allowed to dispose of any newspaper to the scrap vendor, or *kabadiwala*. He would first carefully mark important news items and it was my job to take cuttings and maintain the files under different headings such as 'Political' and 'General.' I had to take clippings and file his news items and weekly columns which had appeared in print. We still have *The Indian Express* Independence Day number. The filing work was tedious and time consuming and was taken for granted. I was my husband's unpaid and, as I thought in my more resentful moods, unacknowledged secretary.

To be accredited to an Indian paper, which would provide him more facilities like a Parliament and a lobby pass, my husband started working for the *Madras Mail*, the newspaper which trained him in journalism. It was a strong rival of *The Hindu*. He wrote a weekly column with the same title, *A Delhi Causerie* by Pertinax, which he had adopted earlier for the *National Herald*. Thanks to the *Madras Mail* he now had contacts with MPs from the South. He came to know and moved closely with leaders like C.N. Annadurai, E.V. Ramaswamy Naickar (Periyar), K. Kamaraj and others. His column, which appeared regularly on Saturdays, was popular and widely read in Madras.

Our home was always littered with newspapers. We were getting six papers every day. It was my job to take cuttings from all the papers. After all the clippings were taken, a pile of newspapers, accumulated over two or three months, would be waiting to be disposed off to the *kabadiwala* along with old bottles. The proceeds from the newspaper sales would be a hundred and fifty to two hundred rupees. I would siphon away this money as small savings, but emergencies invariably arose and my petty cash would be touched. I wanted to protect my small savings by opening an account in my name just to deposit the two hundred odd rupees that I received once in three months. Unfortunately, I did not know how to go about the task.

Around this time, my eldest sister-in-law Krishnambal and her husband Balathimber came to Delhi on a visit. The next lot of newspapers were sold when they were staying with us and I complained that I did not know how to open an account to deposit the sum. Balathimber told me that opening an account was no problem and that he would come with me to the bank and help me do it. He was as good as his word and at last I had an account of my own into which I could deposit the money obtained from selling old newspapers. When my husband came to know about my brand new account he was furious. He scolded and berated me for wanting to have a separate account. He made me go back to the bank and close it at once.

I was deeply hurt and humiliated especially because I could not understand the cause of his red-hot fury. At that time I was very angry and resented my husband's attitude. What could I do but weep my heart out, put on a long face, and then accept my lot and keep muttering to myself in the kitchen.

Looking back I wonder how I could accept so much private hurt and public humiliation without any visible protest. Not that I did not protest, but my anger did not extend beyond gritting my teeth while doing my routine cooking or making a little more noise with my pots and pans than usual. I think I could not have protested in any other way because I lacked economic independence. Like many other women of my generation, I had willy-nilly to bow to my husband's wishes because I was simply a housewife with no independent source of income. The storms in life blew over and our marriage lasted fifty-seven years, but some of those wounds still rankle.

We did a lot of entertaining. Friends from Ceylon would visit us. My husband had close contacts with the Ceylon High Commission and had friends among the staff. Mr Elmore Seneveratne, Deputy High Commissioner, was a good friend of ours. Mr and Mrs Seneveratne would drop in quite often for a chat. We had invitations to diplomatic functions held by the High Commission. There were many other Sinhalese who were close friends. We were also local guardians to some Jaffna Tamil students studying Home Science in the Lady Irwin College. Also by virtue of his accreditation to the *Mail*, my husband and I were invited to all the official Government of India functions. Pressmen had the privilege of taking their wives to these parties.

Once I went with my husband to a tea party for the press hosted by President Dr Rajendra Prasad. It was soon after the post-Partition communal riots. The talk was all about the ghastly incidents in the riots. When I first began accompanying my husband to these official parties, I used to be a little awed by the presence of bigwigs and sophisticated women dressed in the latest style. But, soon I learnt to hold my own. I remember attending an official dinner given by President V.V. Giri to a visiting dignitary. My father knew the President very well, as Mr Giri was an expert on labour relations. All the invitees were lined up and introduced to the President and the Chief Guest by the President's ADC. When my husband was introduced as the foreign correspondent of the *Daily News*, my husband told Mr Giri that I was Mr A.S. Narayanan's daughter. My father was well known for his skill in labour relations and the many negotiations he had done on behalf of plantation labourers. Mr Giri patted me and said, 'Oh, a chip of the old block!'

My husband was a Political Correspondent, so he moved closely among the politicians and ministers from the North and South. Soon he discovered that many of the men idolized by the public had feet of clay. All of them without exception were publicity crazy. Even Pandit Nehru used to brief official photographers before royalty or Presidents of other countries came to India. The cameras duly clicked the casual act of putting an arm around a great personage or certain studied gestures. My husband once interviewed Mrs Indira Gandhi when she was Congress President. Her Secretary Upadhyaya had allotted ten minutes for the interview. But it lasted 45 minutes. Mrs Gandhi was astute in answering questions, but was also alert in taking in new ideas and suggestions. Mr Ramaswamy asked her during the course of the interview, 'Madam, why don't you have a group of at least ten Congressmen around you who are trustworthy and on whom you could rely, enabling you to attend to more important matters?' Mrs Gandhi's reply to this was: 'Mr Ramaswamy, where can I find ten such people?'

Life was interesting, and my husband, being a freelance journalist, had more time to spend with his family. We used to go for night shows at theatres in Connaught Place, after putting the children to bed and locking the front door from the outside. The door to the Ramayyar portion of the house was kept open.

There was a major crisis in the family. This happened when my fourth daughter Tara was a baby of six months. I had bathed and fed the child and given her to the servant, a grown-up fellow, to take care of her. My husband had his lunch and went to office. I called for the child and found the servant pale and shivering with fright. The child was vomiting and unable to cry.

I got so frightened that I called Mrs Ramayyar from next door, and she tried some home remedies for stopping the vomiting. The child was losing consciousness. We called in Dr (Mrs) Goel from Lodi Colony. She and her husband, also a doctor, came on their motorbike and they rubbed brandy on her chest and gave an injection. The child's pulse had dropped to an alarming level. It was only by God's grace that after some time her pulse steadied and heartbeat became normal.

When my husband came home in the evening, he was very worried and thought we should call in a specialist, our family doctor Dr Dawar being out of station. He brought home Dr Dhanda, a heart specialist in Daryaganj. Dr Dhanda was one of the best doctors in Delhi and was physician to the President.

It was curfew time. My husband had a press pass and was able to drive his car in the night. Dr Dhanda came home and after a careful examination said that the child must have hit her head against something hard and there had been an internal haemorrhage, which mercifully had stopped, otherwise it would have been fatal. He called the servant and gave him a thorough warning. He even threatened to call the police if he did not tell us what happened. The man confessed that the child had hit her head against the pillar, while he was playfully running up and down the verandah with the child on his hip.

I discovered the location of the haemorrhage through a most curious incident, though it might invite incredulity. I was a great devotee of Sai Baba of Shirdi and observed a fast every Thursday, a day considered auspicious for Baba. One afternoon I had the baby on my lap and was softly caressing her head. She had become very slow in her responses, and I prayed to Baba fervently for the good health of my daughter. Suddenly I encountered a slightly caved-in portion of the head, which felt soft and squashy. When the doctor was called in he confirmed that this was indeed where the child was hit, and he began treating it. Our family doctor, Dr Dawar, removed the blood clot (haematoma) on the head surgically.

It took more than a year for the child to become normal. Her eyes had developed a terrible squint and it took a long while before she could focus them again and start to recognize us. Tara grew up to be a tall and healthy girl. She now teaches in a college, is happily married, and has a son and a daughter.

Mani, my husband's younger brother, got married in 1946. He had joined Mr Shanti Prasad Jain, who was a son-in-law of R.K. Dalmia, of the Sahu Jain Group of Industries, as his Secretary. He was given a handsome salary and large perks. His two younger brothers, Lakshman and Sundaram, joined him in Calcutta for their further studies. My parents-in-law wound up the Trivandrum establishment, rented out the house, and came away to Calcutta with their youngest daughter Sarada.

Mani had no children. He was a loving and generous person, and looked after the whole family, not only his own brothers and sisters, but also his nephews and nieces and relatives. In fact, anyone who needed help could come to him.

My parents-in-law came to Delhi to stay with us. My father-in-law, an epicure in his tastes, was proud of his son. He had several friends in Delhi, old Travancoreans staying with their sons who were in high positions, and he was in the habit of boasting about his journalist son to these friends. He would secretly take some of Ramaswamy's published articles to proudly show them to his friends. My husband, when he came to know of this, was embarrassed and begged his father not to do it in the future. On top of that, my father-in-law was an admirer of the English language. Once my husband took him to a lecture by Anthony Eden at the Constitution Club. It was soon after Independence, and people had not quite forgiven the British. After the speech the only applause was from my father-in-law, who was quite carried away by Eden's command over the English language! My husband was naturally wincing. My parents-in-law went back to Calcutta to stay with Mani, as it was more convenient there, and the climate was better suited to them than Delhi's extremes of heat and cold.

In Taikad, Trivandrum, the walls of the library / study of my father-in-law's house were lined with almirahs filled with books. He contributed to a London Book Club—the celebrated Foyle's—and two new books would arrive at Taikad on a monthly basis. He possessed the entire set of *Everyman Publications*, the *John of London* literary magazines, the *Strand*, *Punch* etc. It was unusual for a house to have such a well-stocked library. After we left Trivandrum, the Taikad house was sold and the lovely furniture sold for a song or given away to relatives. Mani, who was working with a business firm and had no time for books, transported some of the good books to Calcutta. My sister-in-law arranged the books beautifully, but never read them. In 1993, after Mani died, the undamaged books were donated to a library in Madurai. Most of them were damaged and moth eaten and had to be thrown away. Among these were books dating back to the eighteenth century. I must add here with considerable sadness that my father-in-law, who had nurtured his fine tastes by running into heavy debts, had to declare himself insolvent. The precious collection of books was scattered or destroyed. My husband slowly and patiently built up his own collection of books, which is with me now.

We went down south in October 1951. My husband came back with the four older children, leaving me in Salem for my fifth confinement. We were hoping it would be a boy this time and we wanted to name him Padmanabha, after my father-in-law. But a daughter was born on November 5, and we called her Padmini. In the meantime, the Ramayyar's had shifted to Rouse Avenue and our things were shifted along with theirs in our absence. The next year my father-in-law passed away. In 1953 we moved to a flat in Sujan Singh Park, which the government allotted to my husband. The allotment was most timely. The Government had just passed a rule that no journalist could share accommodation with senior officers of the Government of India. This was to prevent official secrets from being leaked out to journalists.

Mr Ramaswamy wrote a letter to the Minister of the Works and Housing Ministry stating that since pressmen were accredited to the Government of India and were, in a way, serving the government by publishing government news and reporting Parliament proceedings, they should be given Government accommodation. This was granted and my husband was one of the first pressmen to get a Government flat. The only other person before him was the famous cartoonist, Shankar. A week after we shifted, my last child and youngest daughter Vijaya was born on 12 May 1953.

The eldest was staying with my parents in Salem to complete her schooling. Manju passed her S.S.L.C. there and then came to stay with us. She did her Intermediate by correspondence from Panjab University. She then went to Calcutta to stay with her uncle Mani and Aunt Meena. She joined a college in Calcutta and passed her B.A.

In 1964, when Lal Bahadur Shastri was Prime Minister, my husband was indirectly instrumental in bringing about a major decision on a sensitive political issue. Earlier when Nehru was the Prime Minister, Nehru had initiated talks with Sri Lanka on the repatriation of Indians from Ceylon and the issue of granting citizenship to those who wanted to stay. Mrs Bandaranaike, Prime Minister of Sri Lanka, had come for talks to settle the issue.

Mr Ramaswamy as Correspondent of the *Daily News* and *Observer* was with the Sri Lankan crowd day and night. The first round of talks was over, and the Sinhalese were jubilant. Lal Bahadur Shastri had agreed to take in a good percentage of the Indians back, and the Sri Lankans were negotiating for more people to be repatriated. Unfortunately, I am not able to give the exact statistics. My husband, who was an expert on Indo-Sri Lankan affairs, knew what this taking back of a large percentage of Indians would imply. Many of them, who had known only Sri Lanka as their homeland, were shocked at the way the Indian side was inveigled into agreeing to the Sri Lankan figures. My husband was so agitated he could not sleep that night. Very early in the morning he went to Kamaraj's house—Kamaraj was respected as a Congress leader—and apprised him of the gravity of the situation. Kamaraj understood the repatriation issue better than Lal Bahadur Shastri, as it concerned Tamils. He asked his secretary G. Rajagopal to fix up an appointment with Mr Shastri at once. Kamaraj, who was aghast at the concessions already made to the Sri Lankans, briefed Shastri. The next day, as usual, Ramaswamy went to the Sri Lankan camp. After the morning talks, the Prime Minister and her advisers returned with grim faces. There was gloom in the Sri Lankan camp. They were at a loss to know what went wrong suddenly just when they were so confident of pushing their case ahead. The role my husband played was not known to anyone.

The flat we first shifted to was 2-A Sujan Singh Park, a one-bedroom flat. After some months we moved to 6-A Sujan Singh Park, a first-floor flat. It was a big apartment with a large drawing and dining room and two large bedrooms. The front balcony overlooked the lawns of the Ambassador Hotel, which was in the centre of the block of buildings. It was interesting to watch the comings and goings from our balcony. This was the home where my children grew from girlhood to womanhood. The girls took care of each other. With Manju away in Calcutta, Lalita was in charge of the brood. She was a disciplinarian who set the tone of her regime by forbidding the younger ones from calling her 'Lalloo', her pet name. They were to address her by the more dignified 'Lalita',. especially when they rushed up to her in school. When not playing station commander, Lalloo was capable of coming up with wild ideas in which she would involve her adoring sisters. Jayashree who was gentle and lovable was her perfect foil. My husband was so protective about his girls that they seldom interacted with the outside world except when in school. At home they lived in a world of their own—sisters, friends, companions. When I saw them, I would be reminded of Louisa Alcott's *Little Women*, a book I loved and read out to my children.

The children went to the Madrasi Higher Secondary School. My husband was earning well, but journalism was a dicey profession that did not provide the kind of job security that government services did. I lived in constant fear of my husband losing his job. The sword of Damocles made it impossible for us to afford a public school education for the children. The Madrasi School was by far the cheapest means of educating the children, with a monthly charge of one rupee per child and a combined donation of twenty rupees! They walked to school and carried their lunch.

My brother Anantha was living near us at Pandara Road. He was an under-secretary in the Ministry of Commerce. My daughters considered it a treat to spend time at their *mama's* house and play with their cousin Raman. To be in tune with his cousins' girlish games, Raman would sometimes wrap a sari and speak in a high pitch. In my mind, I can still see Raman, the youngster, and the Raman at Chennai in July 2001, still and silent. Raman had passed away in his sleep. He slipped away from us, perhaps to keep his tryst with his childhood playmate Jayashree.

Jayashree's sudden illness was the most devastating thing that happened to us during those otherwise happy years. Jayashree was seven years old when she developed a high temperature suddenly along with a rapid pulse rate. Dr Dawar called in Dr Dhanda for a second consultation and they diagnosed rheumatic fever. It took her more than a year to recover fully. For a few months, we did not want her to go up and down the staircase, so her father would carry her down and drive her to school. In the evening, he would pick her up from school and carry her up the stairs. Jayashree was so sensitive about people seeing her being carried that she would refuse to come unless I went ahead to check that no one was watching us. But, she recovered completely and went on to do her M.A. and became a lecturer in a college.

Jayashree married a Chartered Accountant. She married and two lovely daughters, but her marriage turned out to be a nightmare. Jayashree, who was so shy and sensitive, found that the entire neighbourhood was talking about her family. Some took her mother-in-law's side; others sympathized with her. The child we had brought up with extra love and care suffered a lot.

In 1962, my beloved brother died of a sudden heart attack.

Somehow when I think of the 1960s, my strongest memory is not just Anantha's death, but the bizarre story of the entry and exit of Panrimalai Swamigal in our lives. The story

I am about to relate is one which has been etched in my memory. However, thirty years or more have elapsed and recall is hazy. Perhaps, the story may not have been included in this narrative, but for the name 'Elmer Gantry' coming to my mind by chance.

The name immediately triggered my memory. That long forgotten era of Panrimalai Swami came gushing out.

I would have thought that my parents would have learnt to be more circumspect in placing complete trust in a person after the experience they went through with Subharaghavayya in Ceylon. They made him a partner in a deal without making enquiries into his antecedents and had to cough out Rs 10, 000 to get rid of him.

Now, my parents fell into the clutches of a Swami, whose spiritual level may not have been high, but who certainly had the power to manifest things. At the mere waving of his hands, he could materialize fruits, flowers and articles like small idols, in fact almost anything. He was one Ramaswamy Pillai and was called Panrimalai Swami, as he belonged to the Dindigal district where a hill is named Panrimalai (in Tamil *Panri* means 'pig' and *malai* means 'hill').

My parents became so devoted to him that the Swami stayed with his wife, son, and daughter-in-law in our house in Salem for more than six months. Almost all the other family members also became his ardent devotees. Later, when there was disillusionment, many of these 'ardent devotees' were vociferous in denouncing him and claimed to have 'known all along that he was a fraud'. But, this was much later. Looking back I marvel that anyone could have attributed any spiritual qualities to him. He was completely illiterate—literacy, of course, is not a prerequisite in spirituality—but he had absolutely no knowledge of religion. He could not converse on any subject intelligently, had neither wisdom nor knowledge to impart. Yet my parents thought of him as God incarnate. The Swami's daughter-in-law delivered in our house, my mother attended on her.

Nothing was lacking from my parents' side—physical service, money or true devotion.

The Swami did gather a crowd around him, as he could perform miracles. He would ask a person to stretch his arm and rub it and there would be perfume on the arm. He could produce *vibhuti* (holy ash) and *kumkum* on a large scale.

Sometime around 1959 or 1960 he came to Delhi. We were at Sujan Singh Park at that time. My husband was the only member of the family who did not subscribe to this madness. In fact, he forbade me from going to Salem to see the Swami, when my parents were insisting that I come and partake of his blessings.

When he came to Delhi accompanied by a band of faithful followers, my parents were among them. He stayed in my brother's house. The Swami welcomed us warmly and called my husband '*mapillai*' (son-in-law). My husband had nothing personal against the Swami, but refused to accept him as a saintly person or guru. As a journalist he was interested in the miracles the Swami performed. News of the Swami's miraculous power spread and people with problems thronged my brother's house. Parents brought their sick children to be healed. My brother Anantha did not believe in God the way others did. At heart he was religious, but shunned all rituals and ostentatious worship. He put up with the Swami only for my parents' sake, and would spend as much of his time as possible in the office and with friends and come home late. My sister-in-law also did not believe in the Swami, but I think she rather enjoyed the family's popularity in the neighbourhood—a direct result of the Swami staying in their house.

Panrimalai Swami had a close disciple staying with him. This was Mr Kamalaswamy, an MP from Madras. He used all his influence and brought many prominent people to see the Swami. They would prefer to come at night, unnoticed.

My husband wrote an article about the Swami in the *Madras Mail*, with exclusive pictures. The story was splashed on the front page. The Swami was pleased with my husband for giving him such publicity. My husband later regretted having written the article as it might have misled people. He also arranged for some Indian and foreign correspondents and a few friends to meet the Swami at our house in Sujan Singh Park.

Before the pressmen came, the Swamiji asked my husband to brief him about them. There was a good turnout and the foreign correspondents were given a fantastic demonstration by the Swami manifesting, for their benefit, out-of-season mangoes, flowers, statuettes of the gods, etc. The foreigners lapped it all up and were thrilled. So far as the miraculous part of it went, it was wonderful to watch.

Among those who came there was one Mr Mundkur, a Mangalorean who was Joint Secretary in a Government ministry. He and his wife brought with them their daughter— a well-built, lovely girl of 17 or 18. She was brought in with chains tied to her legs (like an anklet), and after coming inside the house, she was tied to a bedpost. The girl was mad and apparently violent, too. I shall never forget that sight. It seems some astrologer had told them that she would be cured by a Sadhu, and since then they had been taking her to holy men. What agony the parents must have gone through, bringing the child to a house full of strangers, to be stared at! Tears were flowing from my eyes when I went to the room where Panrimalai Swami was sitting and told him about the girl and the parents who wanted him to see her.

The man brushed aside my request without even a sympathetic hearing. He was more interested in asking my husband if that tall foreigner over there was an important person. I was shocked and disgusted; this man was not even a good human being, let alone a Swami! He saw the girl later and told her parents that it was her *Prarabdha Karma* (fate), and nothing could be done about it.

We had sold our Morris Minor as it was now too small for our family and bought a second-hand Hindustan. My parents wanted to take the Swami to Haridwar and Rishikesh by car. The car had just come home, and we were taking it out for the first time. The Swami did some puja and put a garland of flowers on the bonnet of the car and smeared *vibhuti* on the front. We left for Haridwar. When we reached Meerut, the car developed engine trouble. We had to wait for three hours for the repairs before the journey could resume. We found that the secret of the Swami's magic was a small tin box that he always carried with him wherever he went. The box was wrapped in a cloth and was always with him. Wherever he might be, every night he locked himself in a room for about an hour. What he did there, nobody knows. Perhaps the secret of his powers was in that box. I have heard of spirits which do the bidding of their masters. The Swami went back, and my husband never met him again.

My brother died of a massive heart attack on 11 June 1962 at the age of 48. A telegram was sent conveying the news to Dindigal, to my father, who was the officiating priest in a Vinayaka temple under instructions from Panrimalai Swami. My father was so agitated, he could hardly think, he went to the Swami and asked his permission to leave immediately. Sri-La-Sri Panrimalai Swami (to give him his full title), without any compassion for a man who had just lost his son, ordered him to complete all the accounts of the temple and then leave. My mother and father travelled for four days before they could reach Delhi. The tragedy and the Swami's callousness were a terrible shock to my aged parents and us.

My brother's son, Raman, had just joined college. He completed his B.A. Honours in Maths from Ramjas College. While he stayed in the hostel, we were his local guardians. My sister-in-law Saroja went back to Madras and has never visited Delhi after her husband's death. Panrimalai Swami paid a second visit to Delhi and Kamalaswamy put him up in an MP's house. He sent word through various people asking my husband to meet him. But, we never met.

Some days after the Swami had left Delhi, my husband received an anonymous letter threatening terrible things which would wipe out our family. The letter was signed 'A Tantric.' I was thoroughly frightened, but my husband just laughed and threw the letter in the bin. It was meant to frighten us, but nothing happened.

My father in his later years experimented with yoga and meditation. He was a regular visitor to the Sivananda Ashram in Rishikesh. Unfortunately, he took to Hatha Yoga and practised it on his own. He filled several notebooks with his spiritual search and his experiences. But, without a proper guru to guide him, his yogic practices led him to a period of hallucinations. He would sometimes talk of angels sitting on his shoulders; othertimes he would become violent, attacking the evil spirits around him with a knife. He was mostly normal and had not lost his senses, but he did have these hallucinatory fits. He passed away in November 1975 at the ripe old age of 82. He was having *uppuma* made by Mamma, and asked for a second helping, but before Mamma could bring it to him he had choked. He died of asphyxiation.

My mother lived for five more years and died in peace. She was a wonderful person. She had never been to school, but could speak English, and was wise and intelligent. She was a great storyteller and my knowledge of mythological stories comes from her. She passed on her fund of stories to her grandchildren as well. My youngest daughter, Vijaya, recalls Anandamma telling her: why Ganesha has an elephant face, the point at which Hanuman puts in a cameo appearance in the *Mahabharata*, and how Dasharatha received the curse that he would die of *putra shoka* or sorrow resulting from separation from his sons. One of the children's favourite stories was about the theft of the *syamantakamani* and why it is considered inauspicious to look at the moon on the fourth day of the waxing period. It is interesting to note that the narration of stories is essentially a woman's tradition and these stories are

narrated, preserved and passed on by women. No wonder they
are called 'Grandmother's Tales.'

Anandamma was a good astrologer. I have never believed
in astrology and would never participate in the astrological
sessions held by my mother. But, I have known of some of her
startling predictions that came true. Many a young man,
desperate for a degree, a career or marriage, had his horoscope
examined by my mother. Her forecasts hardly ever failed, and
she earned the eternal gratitude of many young men and
women. She had told me years ago that Vijaya would have a
very late marriage and an unusual one. Vijaya got married at
the age of 44 and her sister Jayashree, through her clairvoyance,
even revealed her husband's name to her. Her husband
proposed marriage on the third day of Jayashree's passing away.
As predicted by Mama, Vijaya is extremely happy and now has
a son. My mother had casually picked up astrology, rather than
being trained in this fascinating art. She foretold accurately
through intuition and seldom went wrong. My father, who
could cast horoscopes so perfectly due to his mathematical
skills, never made a single prediction in his life!

I remember how my mother used to get up at 3 o'clock
in the morning in Kandy and sit down for prayers. She had a
clay idol of Krishna and as long as she lived she performed puja
before it. After she passed away, the idol went to my brother
Anantha's wife Saroja. Her grandchildren simply adored her.

In January 1963, we shifted to 17 Bharati Nagar and stayed
in this house for nearly 30 years. The growing years of my six
children were also the years that saw my husband at the peak
of his career. Lalloo and Tara learnt music with a master who
came home to train them, while Padmini learnt dancing from
the Kalakshetra artist, Lalita Kameshwar. My husband took keen
interest in our daughters' progress in music. He was also a well-
known patron of Carnatic music and encouraged upcoming
artists. Seshagopalan, a leading musician of today, sang at a
chamber concert in our house. So did Mani Krishnaswamy,

Gomati Ramasubramaniam and Lakshmi Ramaswamy, who have all become established musicians.

In order to experience singing in harmony with violin and *mridangam*, my husband arranged monthly concerts at home for Lalita and Tara, who were gradually getting to be known in musical circles as the Delhi Sisters. Iswara Iyer, who went on to become a family friend, played the *mridangam* while Lakshminarayana Shastri played the violin. Both were employed in All India Radio. The Delhi Sisters broke up after Lalita got married, but Tara went on to become a B artist of All India Radio and a concert singer.

Where was I during all this? I shared the excitement of the musical soirees, but every such evening left me feeling exhausted. We could not afford to employ a cook, and I ended up spending hours in the kitchen, cooking lunches and making tiffin for my innumerable guests, whose musical appreciation went hand in hand with their appetite for large quantities of *idli-sambhar* and *kesari*. Many insatiable lovers of music stayed on for dinner as well.

Apart from musically inclined guests, we also had politicians, journalists and other intellectuals dropping in to share our meals. My husband would call me up from somewhere and give me an hour to whip up a sumptuous lunch, complete with dessert. Extending our hospitality to utter strangers was not a new thing. I remember an occasion when we had gone to Haridwar and Rishikesh on a holiday. A gentleman from Kerala had come there with his large family on an LTC holiday. They wanted to do some sightseeing in Delhi and were asking my husband for a good place to stay for a week. Overwhelmed by the bonhomie, my husband invited all of them to come and stay with us. With eight of us already at home and six more people added, my life was an unending nightmare of cooking and cleaning, planning attractive menus, and cleaning and cooking! When I was narrating my routine of those days to Vijaya, she recalled a passage from Virginia Woolf's *Room of*

One's Own. I found in it such a perceptive account of my own
life that I would like to reproduce it here:

> 'And if one asked her, longing to pin down the moment
> with date and season, "but what were you doing on the
> fifth of April, 1868 or the second of November 1875",
> she would look vague and say that she could remember
> nothing. For, all the dinners were cooked, the plates and
> cups washed, the children sent to school and gone into
> the world. Nothing remains of it. All has vanished. No
> biography or history has a word to say about it.'

Recalling and recounting events and people over a period
of five decades is a difficult task. Just when I think I have
covered almost all the important events and important
people—a name comes up and with it an entire association of
memories.

It is our friend Meemanage. His full name was Meemanage
Narcissus Anthony Fernando. He was a Sinhalese Roman
Catholic and was trained to enter priesthood. Owing to a
'conscience clause', even though he had taken his perpetual
vows, he chose to get dispensation from the Apostolic Delegate
residing in India and left the Church.

He went back to Colombo and was part of the gay
fashionable society of young men. He was gifted with a talent
for music and had a flair for literature. Somehow he suddenly
got tired of this fashionable life and broke away completely and
became a Buddhist, adopting the name Narcissus Ananda
Mangala. He came to India and was chosen President of the
Ceylonese Union in Mysore in 1942–1943.

Another big change came over him at this stage, and he got
attracted to the movement led by Mahatma Gandhi. He started
wearing *khaddar* (hand-woven cloth) and learnt Hindi. Life
became austere. He came into contact with some eminent
Gandhians like Rafi Ahmad Kidwai, the Kripalanis, and G.V.

Mavlankar. Meemanage became greatly attracted to Nehru's political philosophy and was an ardent admirer of his. He participated in all Congress programmes and even led a Youth Congress delegation to a Conference of World Democratic Youth in Calcutta.

It was after 1948 that my husband met him, and they kept in close touch. He would come home almost every day. As long as he was actively connected with the Congress, he had kept himself busy. After Independence, Pandit Nehru became Prime Minister and a busy man. Meemanage was at a loose end; all his old Congress friends were office-bearers and were too busy to see him. He threw in his lot with a Cambodian monk, venerable Dhammavara, who had an ashram near the Qutab Minar and his own system of nature cure. Meemanage was without money and would find it difficult even to pay for bus fares. He was a regular visitor at our house, and would come in the morning and stay on till dinner. My husband would give him money for his expenses and in winter gave him his own coat and a pair of shoes. He was an interesting talker and he and my husband would spend hours talking.

His training in Sabarmati Ashram made him a champion of the poorer class of Sinhalese in Delhi. He would take up their cause to the High Commission of Ceylon and campaign for greater consideration for them. He became a kind of spokesperson for anyone from Ceylon who had a grievance. The High Commission was not there to accommodate Meemanage and sometimes put him off rudely.

Meemanage once sat on *dharna* in front of the Ceylon High Commission along with a Sinhalese seeking redress. When the Prime Minister of Ceylon, Mr S.W.R.D. Bandaranaike, came on a visit to New Delhi, the High Commission threw extravagant parties at which liquor flowed freely and there were drunken revelries. Meemanage protested against the wasteful expenditure by the High Commission and their refusal to help the poor Sinhalese. Even his petition to Mr Bandaranaike went unheeded. He became a disillusioned and bitter man. He would come home and give vent to his feelings in front of his friend, Ramaswamy, who would try and calm him down. My husband's persuasions were of no avail.

Meemanage decided to teach Prime Minister Bandaranaike and the Ceylon High Commission a lesson. During these outbursts of anger he would write letters to the High Commissioner, Sir Edwin Vijeratne, threatening to expose him. Every day a missile would go from Meemanage to Sir Vijeratne, and the latter would reply promptly, justifying his actions. This went on for some time. My husband knew about these letters as they were written from our house, were shown to him and were posted against his advice. My husband had at that time an occasion to meet Sir Edwin Vijeratne in his house. Lady Vijeratne studied in the same school in Kandy in which I had studied, and both Sir Vijeratne and Lady Vijeratne would often call us over for tea. On that occasion when we went to their house, Sir Edwin was looking ill and unhappy. When my husband remarked on this, he unburdened himself and said, 'That fellow Meemanage is making my life miserable', and he showed him a pile of letters received from him. My husband was silent for a while and then told him, 'But, Sir, why do you have to reply to him? Just throw the letters in the waste paper basket unopened.' Sir Edwin sprang from his chair with a new vigour and said, 'I say, Ramaswamy, what a solution— I never thought of this—you South Indian Brahmins are so brainy.'

While driving back home, my husband and I had a good laugh. He was not sorry for Meemanage, as he had repeatedly asked him to desist from being a nuisance. Meemanage's revenge was complete only after he became a Buddhist monk, Bhikku Ananda Mangala. During the next visit of Mr Bandaranaike, the High Commission arranged a *Dana,* or food offering, to Buddhist monks. The monks were seated in a row and both the Prime Minister of Ceylon and Ceylon's High

Commissioner in India had to bow down before him and offer him the food. Ramaswamy was attending the function and Meemanage looked at him with a triumphant smile. He might have taken to the yellow robe to spite Mr Bandaranaike and Sir Edwin, but he eventually evolved into a truly spiritual monk.

Meemanage once went to Singapore and came back with a Sony Spool type tape-recorder (the small cassette tape recorders had not yet come in the market). He wrote to Pandit Nehru asking him to instruct the Customs Officer to waive the duty. Nehru wrote back to him that he could not do that, but would himself pay the duty for the tape recorder. When he left for Singapore next, he gave that tape recorder to us.

He settled down in a monastery in Singapore and had many male and female devotees. He made frequent visits to India, but now he travelled in comfort and stayed in a 5-Star hotel. He never failed to visit us and bring us presents. On one of these visits my husband arranged for a talk by him on AIR. The Venerable Ananda Mangala wrote out the speech at our house and rehearsed it before us. He had a beautiful voice and a clear English diction. The speech was very good, but unfortunately the reviewer in the *Statesman* referred to him as a person who reminded one of Friar Tuck (the fat and merry monk in *Robin Hood*).

He wrote several letters from Singapore addressing Mr Ramaswamy as 'My dear friend, guide and philosopher.' He died in Singapore, sitting in the lotus pose of the Buddha in meditation. His devotees discovered many references to Ramaswamy in his diary and wrote to my husband about it.

Another friend from Ceylon was Ananda Samarakone. He was a dark man, almost sickly looking, and humble owing to his poverty. He was a highly talented person, a poet and a painter. He became close to my husband and would often drop in at our house. Ramaswamy helped him make some contacts, and an exhibition of his paintings was held at the old

Constitution House. He was something of an idealist and refused to sell his paintings to commercial buyers who offered a good price, in spite of being in great financial distress. The sale of his songs to gramophone companies brought him a little money. It is ironical that Ananda Samarakone, who lived and died in poverty, gained recognition posthumously as the author of Ceylon's national anthem, 'Namo Namo Maatha.'

The marriage of four of my daughters took place in Bharati Nagar beginning with Manju's in 1969. My third daughter Jayashree's marriage was conducted in Calcutta along with my mother-in-law's 80th birthday celebrations in 1971. My mother-in-law lived to be 94.

Jayashree is no more. When I began writing in 1992, soon after my husband had passed away, it was Jayashree who inspired me to write 'something, anything' rather than while away my time in Shimla. I am still writing the book I began, but Jayashree passed away in 1998 due to severe cardiac asthma. She had barely crossed fifty. Her husband was not around during her last moments. With Jayashree, a part of me died.

Writing about Jayashree is like opening wounds afresh, but despite the pain I must write about her. Everyday in the papers I read of so many Jayashrees being burnt to death for not bringing in sufficient dowry, being tortured by the husband and in-laws, but it was only when it happened to my Jayashree that the deaths of these girls began to connect. Jayashree's tragedy is not an uncommon one. The emotional and physical battering of a young bride in India is de regem, but knowing it exists does not make the crime less heinous or the pain less agonizing.

Jayashree's mother-in-law was the sister of my eldest son-in-law. We had celebrated Manju's marriage on a grand scale because my husband's brother Mani, who was childless, regarded Manju as his daughter and wanted to have her wedding on a lavish scale. The ostentation at Manju's marriage sent the wrong signals to my son-in-law's sister, who was suddenly keen on having Jayashree as her daughter-in-law. Her son Rajamani and Jayashree were encouraged to meet, with her acting Cupid. Jayashree was an attractive girl, and her father used to say that she had a million-dollar smile. She was also earning well as a lecturer in Political Science in Janaki Devi Mahavidyala. The demands began the moment the formal engagement took place. We were already financially drained after two marriages and, therefore, were both mentally and financially unprepared. The demands, which began with silver vessels, culminated in a diamond ring for the groom just a few weeks before the marriage. We could not and did not want to fulfil these demands because my husband was in principle opposed to the idea of giving dowry. Friends and relatives patched up the situation and the marriage took place.

For about a year after her marriage, we did not know that Jayashree was unhappy and being ill treated. Jayashree's husband was fond of his beautiful, talented wife and that became a crucial cause of her mother-in-law's vehement hatred towards her. Perhaps her own unconscious frustrations had a role to play since the lady had been married to a widower fourteen years her senior when she was young. Whatever the cause, the result was mental torture. Jayashree did not tell us anything till one night she called home and sobbed, 'Appa, take me away from here.' Despite my husband's assuring her that she would have our backing even if she left her husband, Jayashree held on to the illusion of her marriage. She gave birth to two girls and it is worth recording that her mother-in-law did not even deign to come and see her grandchild when she was born. Perhaps she would have come if my daughter had given birth to a boy. Jayashree had to resign her lecturer's post because of her domestic unhappiness. Her suffering broke our heart, and we decided that our other girls need not go through the pain of marrying into a traditional Brahmin family if they did not want to.

Jayashree's suffering did not go in vain. She believed that her mother-in-law was instrumental in turning her mind to God and putting her on the spiritual path. She had no rancour towards her or her husband. As a result of her inner awakening, Jayashree who was not expressive earlier suddenly began to pour forth spiritual poetry. She wrote these poems in English, chaste Tamil and faultless Sanskrit, despite the absence of a grounding in Tamil and Sanskrit. She reached a state of equanimity where happiness and suffering both appeared to be impostors. Jayashree also had clairvoyance and clairaudience. She could also cure peoples' ailments through her touch though she never cared to cure herself of the asthma that was the psychosomatic reflection of her marital unhappiness.

During the last years of her life, Jayashree stayed separately with her children. Lalloo who lives in Canada gave her house in Delhi to Jayashree. Her husband used to look her up once in a while. This memoir is dedicated to Jayashree who had begged me not to grieve for my husband, but to write down my memories of the past for the sake of my children and grandchildren. She saw what I had written and was happy. On 19 January 1998, Jayashree passed away in my home in Vijaya's arms. One of her predictions came true soon after. Vijaya had crossed forty when Jayashree had told her the name and description of the person she would marry and predicted the birth of her son. Krishnan proposed to Vijaya the third day after Jayashree had passed away. The birth of their son Vijay Krishna has proved the power of Jayashree's words. This is not the only miracle my darling child performed, but I do not want to think of her as a spiritual figure. To me she will always be the child that suffered the most and died young.

My husband did not have a head for finance, nor did he attach much importance to money. He would often say that money was the only commodity one could afford to lose. So it was an achievement for him when he invested in a 500-square yard plot in Greater Kailash I. He bought this land from DLF

Ltd. Initially we had no intention of building a house, but then an ordinance was promulgated that those who owned housing plots should build houses within five years of purchasing the land. This propelled us to start building our house. It took us two years to complete with frequent breaks resulting from lack of funds. But, by borrowing from close friends and against our insurance policy and after selling some property we had down south, we managed to complete the castle of our dreams. S 492 A Greater Kailash was a beautiful house with a drawing and dining room and four bedrooms each with an attached bathroom on the ground floor; the pattern was repeated on the first floor. It was tastefully designed, without any ostentatious marble or elements of grandeur.

But, the house was built with such labour only to be sold two years later for exactly the cost we had incurred. My husband who was Vice-President and then President of the Press Association had framed certain rules and guidelines for journalists. Among the rules he had laid down was one that forbade pressmen from letting out their own house while occupying government accommodation. Many of the journalists had their own house let out at a profit and were occupying government flats allotted to them as accredited press correspondents. This rule did not meet with their approval, and Mr Ramaswamy was not elected for a second term.

Since we lived in a centrally located area with schools and colleges at an accessible distance, we did not shift to our own house and because of the rule my husband had helped frame we did not let out the house. Finally, the house was sold to a businessman from Calcutta who had negotiated for the sale a few months earlier and had insisted on giving a token Rs 101 as an advance. He neither wrote nor came to meet us for four months. By this time the boom in real estate had begun and houses were fetching phenomenal prices. There were higher offers for our house, but my husband stood by his commitment to the Calcutta businessman and wrote to him to relieve him of the agreement to sell the house to him. Within a week of our sending him the letter, the man came to Delhi and my husband concluded the sale of the house for the agreed price. Like Lord Rama his motto was, 'Pran jaye par vachan na jaye' meaning 'One's word, once given, will be honoured even under pain of death.' Needless to say all my tears and pleadings to at least ask for a higher price went unheeded. We also needed the money for the marriages of the younger girls. The house was sold just before Jayashree's marriage. Marriages for Tara and Padmini followed within a few years. Vijaya got married only last year when she was past forty.

Through the years of turbulence that marked our autumnal years, I never gave up my thirst for education. Right through feeding and taking care of my babies in their early years to teaching and grooming them into womanhood, I continued to study. It is my opinion that the growing process in human beings varies from individual to individual. One cannot apply Shakespeare's seven stages of man to everyone. I was never the whining schoolgirl going unwillingly to school. On the contrary, I was enthusiastic about school and studies. Even at that early age, I was a voracious reader and read Charles Dickens, Thomas Hardy, Walter Scott and Jane Austin and many other authors popular at that time.

My husband was a great believer in women's education and wanted all his daughters to have the highest qualification. He used to tell Vijaya, 'You are a scholar first and a woman later.' He also planned that they should take up teaching as a profession and not go into the civil service and become 'a pen-pushing bureaucrat.'

Surprisingly, however, he never took my thirst for knowledge and my desire to educate myself seriously. It all came to a head when a friend of ours, an Air Force officer, brought his wife to our house and wanted my husband's advice regarding the course of study she should pursue. She was keen on doing her M.Phil in Sociology. My husband was quite enthusiastic and arranged a table and chair for her in our study room. He brought books from the Central Secretariat library and Parliament library for her to study. Of course, I provided her with meals. My heart burnt with resentment. I was hurt and unhappy to see my husband's enthusiasm for Nirmala's education, while his enthusiasm for my own burning desire for knowledge was so glaringly amiss.

I wanted to take a Punjab Matriculation exam to qualify for a degree course, and my brother even gave me a guide book for coping with mathematics. My husband, however, gave me no encouragement. On the contrary, my books were promptly given away to my youngest sister-in-law, who was not even interested in academics. I had to give up my study only because I could not take time off from the kitchen, housework and children. Education in my case was considered irrelevant.

I realize that the growing process was slow for me. I was a romantic, playful and imaginative child. That is why I have deep empathy with Walter Mitty. Building castles in the air and dreaming of living in them is my secret dream. There was a gap of eleven years between my husband and me. I went to him when I was just thirteen years and three months. Perhaps this was what made my husband so protective towards me. I had just entered my teens, and there was still so much of laughter and playfulness in me waiting to burst out. But, in my in-laws' house I had to behave like a grown up, married woman, solemn and modest all the time, while I would be itching to giggle and had to suppress myself with great effort. I had to wear a nine-yard sari, which would often become loose, since I hadn't yet developed a figure with womanly contours. My husband had to teach me many things. Coming from a convent school background had made me somewhat westernized in my habits. I could not drink anything without sipping from the tumbler. The South Indian Brahmin way of drinking from a tumbler was to pour the liquid down the throat without touching the tumbler with the lips, as it would then have become *saliva*-polluted. It took me some time to master this art. I would usually hide behind a door or pillar and quickly sip in large draughts. It was entirely a new way of life for me, and I was sometimes miserable, missing the things I was used to. My husband was understanding and would talk me out of my blues.

Perhaps it was the protective attitude he had adopted and the responsibility of bringing me up like a child which persisted in him even after I became a mother. I know my husband was passionately in love with me, but that did not make him blind to what he thought were my serious failings. Even as a mother of six daughters, I never had the right matronly attitude or exercised any discipline over the children. I was not an efficient housewife and did not run a neat and orderly household. This was partly due to my husband's profession with no fixed hours for meals and so on and also partly due to my being unable to organize myself in getting things done. I would uncomplainingly manage without essential provisions. Bringing up the girls was not an easy task. They were too young to help me in housework and sometimes meals were not ready in time. Often my husband's hairbrush and comb were not kept in their place, books from his table would have been taken away by the kids, his pens would be missing and the list of my many lapses would keep on piling.

One day my husband was so angry with me over one such trivial thing that he punished the children by making them sit facing the wall. When I protested, he made me also sit with them. I was furious, but my fury only led to tears. His anger soon cooled down, and he was contrite and tried to make it up to me in many ways, but the incident still rankles.

It was 1964 and on September 24, I completed forty years. I got married when I was ten and my schooling ended when I was thirteen. Two things hurt me very much: not being able to learn music and not continuing my studies. But, how could one do anything creative when there was a large family to be looked after and relatives and guests kept coming? On top of all that we kept an open house and food had to be available for the casual visitors and my husband's circle of journalist-friends. After a sincere effort, I gave up. This feeling of frustration was ever within me, and I was determined that some day I would make my life meaningful.

Perhaps these were thoughts which influenced me when I read Pearl S. Buck's *Pavilion of Women.* The main theme was that the lady, who was the head of the Chinese family, decided on her fortieth birthday to be independent of her husband's physical needs and presented him with a young girl for a wife. The only idea, which appealed to me from the story, was the 'becoming independent' part. I was not prepared to abdicate either my wifely duties or my usefulness in the family, but the book helped me to make a resolution on my fortieth birthday. This was a formal declaration to myself to the effect that from henceforth I would do what I liked and would make my own decisions. It took me 40 years to take that decision, whereas today even a child has the courage to make its own choices.

My husband was a truly loving person, but having seven females to care for (six daughters and a young wife) made him take his responsibilities somewhat too seriously and shaped him into an autocrat. I used to jocularly call him The Benevolent Dictator. From choosing the subjects the girls should study, to choosing their dresses and later on their saris, his opinion prevailed. Sweetly and gently, but firmly, he ruled the family.

In making the announcement in a romantic manner, in my mind I was imitating the Chinese lady of Buck's novel. But, no one knew this and my husband thought I was rebelling against his authority and was learning to be a feminist. I have a feeling that he never forgave me for this sudden change of character. I did not become a rebel nor did I flout any of his rules. I carried on in the same way, continuing the immense task of managing a large household.

But, I had changed in one significant way. I took up my *veena* playing in earnest. I practised for hours and also took music lessons from V. G. Subramanian, a top All India Radio artist. He was a Wing Commander in the Indian Air Force and came from a family of musicians. I did achieve a certain measure of proficiency in playing the *veena*.

Then I taught myself Telugu and Kannada. My aim was to learn all the four major languages of the South: Tamil (I already knew), Telugu, Kannada, and Malayalam. I could not achieve much in this sphere and only gained a smattering of the three languages. I also learnt to write and speak Sanskrit and used to travel by bus, all by myself, to attend a Sanskrit Speaking Camp.

When I was a child someone asked me, 'What do you want to be when you grow up?' My reply was that I would like to marry and have a large family. My children would have only sweets, cakes and ice cream for lunch and dinner. They could play all the time, and I would never scold them. I suppose this was the logic behind my indulgence towards my children. I would tell them stories, teach them and play with them. I remember inventing a story for them while giving them an oil bath. It went like this: 'The head was dirty and the enemy was dirt, the oil came to fight the dirt, but the oil should not think it could occupy the head permanently—no, not at all. The oil had an enemy called *shikakai* (soapnut powder), and it came and drove away all the oil. But the *shikakai* was mistaken if it thought it had a permanent home on the head—no, not at all. It had an enemy called water. So the water came and drained off all the *shikakai*. "Aha" thought the water, "now I can make myself comfortable here." But no, not at all. A big towel came and wiped off all the water. Now, you can see the hair is clean and lovely.'

I would teach them the English songs I had learnt at school. I remember telling them the lines our school principal, Ms.

Mallet, included in her speech on the Annual Day. I asked the girls to repeat it after me: 'Lipstick, rouge and painted nails are a vulgar extension of the female personality.'

My husband took them in hand once they were old enough to understand literature and poetry. We had reading sessions of Shakespeare, Goldsmith and almost all the poets. He would also read from Tagore's *Gitanjali*. Every New Year's eve, all of us sat around him, and he would read out from a book till midnight. After ushering in the New Year, there would be a round of 'Happy New Year' greetings, exchanged. At these sessions I would invariably fall asleep. The fatigue after the day's work and the sonorous voice of my husband would have a soporific effect on me.

After his retirement from active journalism, my husband took up residence in a cottage in Madras where he could sojourn for the winter to do his writing undisturbed. He was there for two winters and two of his novels were written there. I stayed with him for just two months, as the Delhi house could not be kept locked. I did not want to leave my youngest daughter Vijaya alone in Delhi either. During those two months I learnt Telugu from our neighbour Mr P.M. Rao, an old gentleman and a scholar in Telugu. He was happy with my progress and was keen on me continuing Telugu studies. But, two months was all the time I had, so I returned to Delhi. My husband gave up the cottage, as it was rented out to him by some women's organization and he was expected to stay throughout the year.

My achievements, despite being small, did give me great satisfaction, though I am aware that in writing a personal narrative of this sort, there is a tendency to put the events in one's life in a favourable light. I had the opportunity of playing in a group called Pancha Veena. We gave performances in all the big halls in Delhi, Ashoka Hotel and Kamani Auditorium to name a few, and even gave a performance in Rashtrapati Bhawan as an accompanist to Indrani Rahman's dance numbers. All this became possible because of my friend and *veena* teacher, Mrs Visalam Venkatachalam, who gave me every encouragement in fulfilling my ambition. This helped me get over my frustration and gave a boost to my self-respect.

With the passing away of my beloved husband in 1992, I left Bharati Nagar and the memories of our life there and moved with my youngest daughter Vijaya to her flat. In September the same year, we moved to Shimla where she had a fellowship. I lost my brother-in-law Mani the next year and within six months of his death another brother-in-law, Lakshman, died. Of the four sons and five daughters in my husband's family, one son and two daughters remain.

The writing of this memoir has given me tremendous pleasure and a lot of pain. I never had the habit of maintaining a diary and whatever I have written has been taken from the storehouse of my memory. While writing, a poem of Lord Tennyson's, *Grandmother*, came to mind. Like Tennyson's grandmother, who remembered with such clarity incidents in her life which happened 70 years ago, I too echo Tennyson's words, 'Seventy years ago my darlings, seventy years ago.'

Seventy Years Ago, My Darling

❧❁❧

Seventy years later I see myself sitting, surrounded by my children, grandchildren and great grandchildren. My family has been a source of pride and joy to me. Of the two pillars of the family—the father and the mother—one has gone, leaving me, the mother, to see the family grow to its present strength.

I sometimes find I am no longer the pillar on which my children and grandchildren lean for strength and advice. I have taken a back seat. Having just entered a new century and a new millennium, I simply watch the younger generation grow up, with their new-found ideas of 'individual space' and 'self-expression.' I find they are much more capable and self-reliant than the youngsters of my generation were. But I cannot help feeling that in discovering their individual freedom, in carving out their own spaces, they distance themselves from the family. They love me, but no longer need me in the way we needed our elders. I found my space within my family and later within my marital home, but youngsters today locate their space outside their family.

As I look at it, in the first half of this century, life was different in that the family played an important role in the upbringing of children. Even when one was old enough to take care of one's own family and children, we still had to take the counsel of our elders. The joint family system was the norm and the nuclear family an exception. Today, it is just the other way around.

In my youth, feminism had not made an appearance on the Indian scene. As I was growing up in the 1920s, women in Britain were agitating for their franchise and were known as suffragettes. In India women were gradually becoming a part of the freedom struggle. I would not call myself a wholly traditional woman since I had a somewhat modern upbringing, including a convent school education although only up to the primary level. I am quite broad-minded in my views and yet there are times when I feel I belong to a different age, especially when I am confronted with the opinions of my grandchildren. I have brought up six daughters and I can proudly say that I have never had any problems with them as teenagers. Like Louisa Alcott's *Little Women,* my children played and argued within the home, within the close-knit family circle. Television was still a novelty, not affordable in many middle class homes, including ours. The computer and Internet were nowhere on the horizon. My husband painstakingly typed his weekly articles and students gathered information in libraries rather than on the Net.

My third daughter Jayashree is now no more. Vijaya got engaged within thirteen days of her sister's death and was married to Krishnan within a month of Jayashree's passing away. My second daughter Lalita, who is settled in Canada, had come for the wedding and when she went back to Toronto, I went with her.

I am concluding these random recollections of my life sitting here in Lalita's beautiful cottage house—5 Patrick Drive, Aurora—a little town 40 kilometres from the bustling metropolis of Toronto. Lalita was not a working woman, but since her husband's death in 1996, she has faced up to the task of continuing the education of her three children with courage, robustness and fortitude. She has rebuilt her life and provided me with this opportunity to travel westwards and reflect on my life from Kandy (Sri Lanka), Trivandrum and New Delhi to Toronto.

My eldest daughter Manju, the little imaginative child I have written about, is now a grandmother, which makes me a great grandmother! She and her husband Mani live with their son in Delhi.

My fourth daughter, Tara, who had an accident-prone childhood, teaches in a women's college. She has a son who is an architect and a daughter, an excellent singer, in college. She also lives in Delhi with her engineer husband, Natarajan.

Padmini, the most enthusiastic and vivacious, is the fifth in line. She is the pivot around whom the family revolves and comes together during all family gatherings. Her capacious house provides the venue for almost all our family functions which are complemented by her innate generosity. She and her husband are both college teachers. They have two girls, one in college and the other still in high school.

Vijaya, my youngest, is the scholar of the family. Apart from being a university teacher, she has authored three books. Though by profession a historian, she has, because of her deep religious faith, done her research on spiritual movements, especially women saints. She is also into Women's Studies. She got married late, but in the most unexpected manner. Her marriage to Krishnan, who like my husband is a freelance journalist and research consultant, has given me the greatest happiness in my life.

Here I am in Canada enjoying the incredible beauty of the suburban town of Aurora. For me, Canada has been a tremendous experience with many firsts. As I jokingly put it to my family: my first plane travel, my first experience of walking on a moving escalator, the departmental stores, the self-filling gas stations, everything computerized, no human touch anywhere, especially in business and commerce—all this is new to me.

I enjoy a lot of leisure, take quiet walks by myself, tend the garden, occasionally socialize with people who are either

friends of Lalita's or my grandchildren's and sometimes with
the small circle of Indians living in the area. During my walks,
I stand before every house I pass and admire the exquisitely
maintained gardens and lawns. Usually, a cheerful voice greets
me with, 'Hello, how are you doing today?' or just, 'Lovely
day, isn't it?' The gardens in spring are a riot of colours and
some are adorned with lifelike statues of animals. The flower
pots came in various shapes and sizes with some shaped like
ducks and others like swans. The beautiful maple trees with
leaves turning from green to golden and red in autumn
dominate the landscape. Some trees are covered with tiny
white blossoms, appropriately named baby's breath. I have
to keep telling myself not to fall in love with this temporary
abode. Soon I shall have go back to my beloved India and
Delhi, with its power cuts, the littered streets, newspapers with
stories of petty corruption and crimes, and the snarling,
crawling traffic of the Capital.

Nevertheless, it is my beloved Motherland, the very
thought of it brings tears to my eyes. I will be back in Delhi
before it begins to snow in Canada.

I end this simple story of my life and times with a sense of
fulfillment and gratitude to God for everything. I recall some
lines of Rita Joe's, the Native Canadian poet:

> My body lay upon the earth floor
> Reality came when I awoke
> Breaking the images of ages before
> In a lost fantasy
> Desires broke without reason.